Dec. 18, 2022

To: Patricia

From one artist to another.

Enjoy!

Bella Adams ♥

The Spirit of the Artist

Zilla

The life and work
of fine artist, Zilla Adams

spectrum art

Copyright © 2017
by Zilla Adams

Published by Spectrum Art
3300 Pebblebrook Drive #58, Seabrook, TX 77586

No part of this publication may be reproduced, nor stored in a retrieval system, nor transmitted in any form nor by any means, electronic, mechanical, photocopying, recording, or otherwise, without written permission of the pubisher and/or the author.

Cover art, "Brilliant Maui Sunset" by Zilla Adams

Design and production by Janice Shay / Pinafore Press

ISBN: 978-0-615-14326-2

Printed in Canada

*This book is dedicated to my beloved maternal grandmother,
Wilma Davis Valentine, fine artist.*

And to my children and grandchildren, the lights of my life.

Kelly Valentine Witherspoon Zabcik	Adam Joseph Witherspoon	Alethea (Ali) Katherine Witherspoon
Robert Zabcik	Jessica Jordan Witherspoon	Mackenzie Mary Riedle
Ryan Robert Zabcik	Avery Jordan Witherspoon	William Witherspoon Anthony
Kathryn Ann Zabcik		Savannah Valentine Witherspoon Anthony

This book is a statement of my truth. As such, it presents my personal perspectives, views, and memories. No two minds on earth ever think exactly alike—varying truths and perspectives are to be expected and, hopefully, respected. I believe that personal opinions and freedom of expression are tools for the artist. If my truth is different from yours, please don't feel offended, because that is not my intention.

I feel the deepest heartfelt gratitude to everone in my life: For the friends, mentors, and loved ones, and for those who taught me the hardest lessons, because those lessons promote acts of forgivness and sprirtual growth. My life has been enriched beyond words.

Mahalo.

| CONTENTS |

Introduction	8
Chapter One: Life Drawings	58
Chapter Two: Portraits	76
Chapter Three: Animals	88
Chapter Four: Florals, Plants	98
Chapter Five: Landscapes	112
Chapter Six: Collages, Mosaics	134
Chapter Seven: Circles	152
Chapter Eight: Abstracts	166
Chapter Nine: Etchings	184
Chapter Ten: Sculptures	190
Chapter Eleven: Pen & Ink, Surrealism	196
Chapter Twelve: Drawing My Story	224
Biographical Information	233
Acknowledgments	240

INTRODUCTION

Introduction

"The unexamined life is not worth living." —SOCRATES

"Curiosity is the main energy." —ROBERT RAUSCHENBERG

It was 1987 and I had only been in Maui, Hawaii, a few days. I had just left my fiancé after two and a half years of living on our sailboat in Key West, Florida. I didn't know it at the time, but I was about to begin a new life. It was a beautiful day and I was very curious to see the harbor in Lahaina Town, the small village on the western shore, where I had landed. I walked through town, relishing the lush tropical flowers and the giant Banyan trees, eager to check out the fabled tall-ship, The Carthaginian, which was moored in the harbor. I crossed the area where the Hawaiian King's Palace once stood and there it was! An antique double-masted sailing ship from the whaling days, floating in the crystal clear Pacific. It was breathtaking! As I studied the details of the rigging, imaginary images of swashbuckling sailors and the ancient Hawaiians filled my mind. "Aloha," a deep voice said, "My name is Caesar." I started and turned to see a tall, muscular and regal-looking Hawaiian man with snow white hair. It was very striking in contrast to his golden brown skin. He was extremely handsome, with jet black eyes and perfect teeth as he smiled.

"Aloha" I said, smiling back, hoping I was pronouncing it properly. His smile lit up his whole face as he asked me my name. "I'm Zilla Adams, and I'm happy to meet you." We admired the ship together and chatted. When I pointed to the elaborate gold pendant around his neck, he confessed that he was descended from Hawaiian royalty and it had been passed down to him by his great grandmother. I could certainly believe that.

He then smiled again and said: "I know your name!" I looked back quizzically and said, "What? (I had just told him.)

He said, "I know your *Hawaiian* name."

I was instantly intrigued and sensed that this was becoming more than a casual meeting. "Ok, then, what is my Hawaiian name?" His eyes twinkled knowingly as he pronounced it slowly and ceremoniously, "A-KE-A-KA-MAI."

"A-ke-a-ka-mai," I repeated, as I paused to let the sounds enter my head. He waited. Then I asked, "What does it mean?" He replied, "Ake means to desire, and Akamai means wisdom, so put together, they mean to yearn for wisdom. If

Caesar, Hawai'ian royalty.

you put Aloha and Akeakamai together, you are a lover of wisdom, a philosopher"! (These words were like the Greek words, Philo and Sophia, when used together also meant philosophy!) My eyes widened and my mouth dropped. I instantly flashed back to the day, at age twelve, when I first read the quote by Socrates: "The unexamined life is not worth living."

As I read those words, they become my mantra, one of the guiding-principles for my life. They also explained why I had always had such a burning curiosity for life.

I stared back at Caesar in awe. How could this total stranger come out of nowhere and give me such an exact name, one that I had carried in my heart all these years? Are the Hawaiians psychic? Or, magic? Or, what?

Caesar could see the impact on my face and he knew that he had struck a chord.

"I'm glad that you are pleased." Then he took my hand and tenderly said, "Aloha." As he turned to leave, I quietly said, "Aloha" and stood still and awestruck. How did this stranger know the guiding principle of my life"?

What Caesar said was true. Even as a toddler back in Austin, Texas, my enormous curiosity drove me to question everything. Most children are curious by nature, but curiosity made me examine life just as Socrates had instructed. It was a passion. I also had a strong intuitive sense, an extra awareness, which I've never lost. I also know that from my earliest memories, I always wanted to be an artist. It was not a wish, but my identity, it was who I was. My mother wrote in my baby book: "Zilla said, "I am an artist" at age 2½ years."

How can that happen? How can a child know such things at such a young age? Where does it come from? Is it a gift? What are the influences? What is that urge to capture the world with paint, or express one's deepest emotions through art?

I guess my first major influence was that I was born into a visually oriented family. My mother, Marjorie Valentine Adams, was an artist and photographer whose work was published in *Look* magazine. My maternal grandmother, Wilma Davis Valentine,

I've arrived on the beach in Lahaina, Maui.

My mother, Marjorie Adams, and me at age seven.

My dad, Louis "Red" Taft Adams, as a young man.

Below, left to right: Grandmother liked to create costumes for me to play dress-up.

was a landscape oil painter, a pianist, and a poet who wrote sonnets, the most difficult poems to write. My dad, Louis "Red" Adams, was a naturalist and environmental filmmaker, who taught me to love the beauty of nature and the outdoors. He was always pointing out beautiful scenes, and teaching me to really observe my surroundings.

I was born on May 6, 1942, and seven months later my dad joined the Navy, volunteering to fight in World War II. Hitler had already gobbled up about 24 countries in Europe, and the USA had rallied. We moved to the Naval Air Station in Corpus Christi, Texas, where dad taught gunnery and artillery to the young sailors who were headed overseas.

This is where I said my first word, "airplane," at seven months old. Upon hearing the roar of the massive airplane engines and seeing those huge monsters flying overhead, I said "airplane" even before I said my own name. My brother, Lew V. Adams, was born there in 1945, the same year the Japanese bombed Pearl Harbor in Hawaii, and the war ended.

We moved back to Austin and to our extended family, where our ancestors had lived for five generations. My great grandfa-

ther, Henry Phillip Davis, had served as a state legislator in the Texas capitol and had brought the impeachment charges against Texas' most corrupt governor. His intellect, ethics and leadership had set standards for the whole family to follow. In our family, we were expected to be accomplished at everything: art, music, dance, writing, sports, science, and even humor. We were expected to be well-rounded and talented, an ideal exemplified in the Renaissance.

Both my parents were excited about life. They were good-natured, happy, busy people who were adventurous and relatively fearless. After the war, back in Austin, they built our new house themselves. Mother had studied Architecture at the University of Texas, and designed our house; and dad, who was a good carpenter, built it. As children, we were expected to have the same "can do" attitudes and high ethical standards.

Our new house was built on property located right next door to my grandparents, so my artist grandmother, Wilma, became one of my favorite people. As her first grandchild, I got special attention. Her house was filled with her oil paintings, which was unusual in many Texas homes. She was really a fun and loving person who delighted in playing dress-up with me. She would create little costumes, put them on me, and take photos. I loved it! She also taught me to paint at a very early age. She even took me to classical concerts when I was only three years old. She kept me quiet by feeding me Lifesavers candy throughout the performance. As a result, I quickly became a lover of classical music. She also read history stories and poetry to me. She was the most unconditionally loving and spiritual person in my life and I adored her.

At Wooldridge Elementary school, I stood out for three reasons. First, I had bright red hair. My mother, father, grandmother, and brother also had bright red hair, so that was rather unusual. Plus, I had a very unique name—Zilla! During all these years, I've never met anyone with my exact name, (which makes it, incidentally, a great name for an artist). In fact, with a name like Zilla, I didn't even need a last name.

The third thing that made me unique was that I could draw really well. Children would ask me to draw pictures for them and I

I was always drawing.

would always sign my name simply "Zilla." Recently, I ran into my old childhood friend, Nancy Smith Norvell, who bragged that she still had some of my drawings from elementary school! Our third grade class had made a book of drawings about American Indians and mine was on the cover, with several inside, too. I asked how she knew it was mine and she said it was signed. She had kept the whole book all these years! I was utterly amazed.

When I was eleven, a very important event occurred. I was accepted into the University of Texas Gifted and Talented Art Program, the Junior Art Project. I was the youngest child to be chosen, and every Saturday I went to classes on campus at the University's art department. I studied life drawing and painting with the

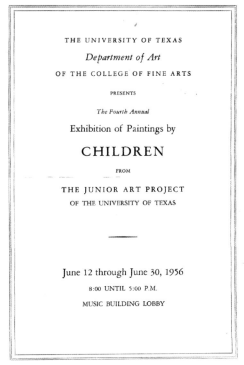

My very first exhibition, at the age of 14.

UT art professors. This catapulted me into an advanced level of study and an attitude that few children had; and it spurred a determination to acquire the skills to be the best I could be. I can still remember the wonderful smells of oil paint and turpentine whenever I walked through that door. It was divine. I studied there for three years.

At the age of twelve, another very wonderful event occurred. On my birthday, my parents gave me a gift which I have cherished all my life. It was a book by Reginald Marsh titled *Anatomy for Artists*, and it launched me into the serious study of human anatomy and figure drawing. As I began to copy all the illustrations, an intense passion for life drawing was ignited. This book also shifted my awareness and self-concept from a child who draws pictures to a serious artist who has a life's quest and a career to pursue.

I also began reading art history and the lives of the famous artists. When I read that Michelangelo had finished sculpting the "David" in his twenties, it gave me hope that I, too, might achieve great things. I did not want to be a cheerleader, a famous singer, nor a movie star—typical aspirations of other girls my age. My dream was to go to Paris and study with the great Picasso, my hero. I wanted to study the art in the Louvre and see the masterpieces in the great museums in Europe. Instead, my family headed south.

When I was thirteen, my mother surprised us with a summer trip to Mexico. We were to leave the day school was out, and return the day before school started in the fall. We planned to drive to Mazatlan on the Pacific Coast in a 1940 Ford that Mom had inherited from her Uncle Walter. It was two years older than I was, and had sat in his garage for 15 years. But it was in mint condition and Mom, who was then a published writer, wanted to sell an article about the trip to FORD Magazine. The editor had bought the idea and advanced her the money to pay for our trip. Hooray! A free trip to Mexico! (Remember, I said my parents were adventurous? Well, a huge adventure was about to begin).

When my grandmother heard this news, she decided to come along in her car, and bring her fluffy white dog, Putsie. Dad had to stay at work, so he planned to join us later during his vacation. My brother Lew and I were excited because we had only left the country for one day, during a camping trip to Big Bend National Park, when I was eight and he was five. We had ridden across the Rio Grande River into Mexico in the silver ore trucks from the silver mines and had eaten at a tiny cantina in the village. That was the extent of our travel abroad.

The Mazatlan trip was a fantastic idea, plus mother spoke fair Spanish, so what could go wrong?

The trip South went fairly smoothly. Lew rode in front with Mom in the '40 Ford, and I was with grandmother and Putsie in her car, behind them. As we moved deeper into Mexico, I began to feel that we were going back in time. We saw women in the fields with babies swaddled in shawls on their backs. They ground corn on rough stones, added water, and cooked tortillas on pieces of tin over open fires. We stopped in villages where the people touched our red hair and then genuflected crosses over their chests. I felt as if they were protecting themselves from some "curse" that we—or our red hair—supposedly carried. That was really weird.

We visited colorful markets with amazing fruits and flowers, and I had my first taste of the most delicious food in the world: mangoes! We had left Elvis Presley gyrating on the TV in America,

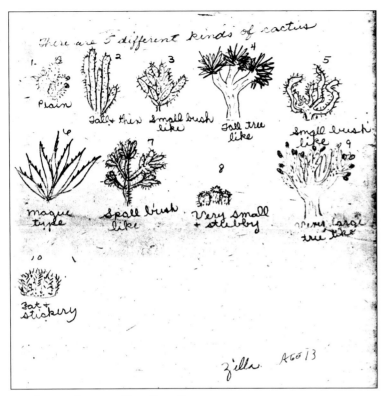

A page from my Mazatlan diary.

and had arrived in a place which seemed much closer to the "real" world, with people much closer to the earth. I felt envious.

Finally, we climbed into the mountains of the Sierra Nevada, on a road with hairpin curves and steep grades. When we were on the east side of the mountain, it was a barren desert. As we reached the west side, it turned tropical and green. That was astounding to me. Finally, as we travelled to much higher altitudes, the roads became narrower and there were no guard rails. Suddenly, mother's car started swerving off the road, left into the oncoming traffic, then swerving right, dropping off onto the narrow shoulder with the cliff's edge just a few inches away. Grandmother started honking frantically as she screamed, "Marjorie! Marjorie! Wake up!" I was screaming and crying as I watched my mom and brother narrowly miss death, second by second. Finally, the car swerved so violently that she woke up. She was dazed, but slowed the car to a stop. We jumped out and grabbed each other. Grandmother quickly realized that Mom was suffering from altitude sickness, which was unknown to us in Texas. We couldn't go on much further until she rested or got medicine. I moved into Mom's car and Lew moved back with Grandmother.

A short distance up ahead we stopped at an adobe house with a barn. We knocked and were greeted by a courteous Mexican lady. She served us soup, and rolls like little bricks which were so hard we couldn't chew, and mother negotiated a place to sleep. She and grandmother stayed in the house and Lew and I stayed in a room in the barn on a straw mattress. The windows had no glass, nor screens. We had a fitful night, but finally we slept.

Suddenly, in the early morning hours, there was a loud screeching sound that blasted us both awake! We screamed and bolted up to see a huge donkey's head poking through the window right in front of our faces. *HEE HAW! HEE HAW! HEE HAW!!!*

Holy Moly! Yet another traumatic experience in this dangerous foreign land!! The women rushed out to see if we were still alive, and we must have looked like we had seen a ghost. It certainly felt like it.

At breakfast, mother ordered a three minute egg, in spite of the woman's protestations, and it arrived looking totally raw. Mother looked suspiciously at the lady until she explained that it takes much longer to cook at high altitudes. Wow! Who knew? This place was definitely more difficult and dangerous than good ole Austin, Texas, but at least we were alive.

We lived in Mazatlan for three months in an apartment overlooking the ocean, swimming every day in our beautiful, beloved Pacific. I kept a diary of all our adventures, even drawing the many kinds of cactus and exotic plants and animals we encountered.

The only hotel in town had a one-story elevator, a pool green with algae, and two huge boa constrictor snakes in the basement to catch the rats. We didn't really believe that they existed, until one day an excited man came and led us into the lobby. There was one large, heavy wooden rocking chair sitting empty and a commotion we could hear in the hall. Suddenly, two men arrived carrying the most enormous snake I had ever seen!

It was so big, it took two men to lift it. We were stunned. After the initial shock, I realized just how beautiful it was, with gold and brown and black colors in marvelous patterns. It's head was about six inches long and if you got too near, it would hiss very loudly. Amazing! I wish I could have painted him.

In my dairy, I listed all the dangerous adventures I had experienced: I rode on a runaway horse that narrowly missed being hit by a train. I was nearly swept away by a powerful under-tow current. I was stung by a Portuguese Man-o-War jellyfish which burned like a hot iron, and, near the lighthouse, a huge hammerhead shark about nine feet long swam right by me. (Fortunately, I thought hammerheads weren't dangerous, so I kept still). On an outing to Guadalajara, I thought I was going to die from "Montezuma's Revenge" (violent diarrhea and vomiting). Then, when dad arrived, we drove deep into the jungle, only to be blocked by six banditos on horseback, with rifles and bandilleros full of bullets strapped across their chests. Dad immediately threw the car into reverse and backed the whole way out of the jungle, as fast as he could. We ended up laughing about it.

Regardless of the scary stuff, this trip ignited a lust for travel deep in my core and stretched my little world view, influencing my life forever. I vowed to go to as many countries as possible. I had seen the ancient Mayan and Aztec art in the National Museum in Mexico City and the colorful and rich folk art in the villages. The beauty of the land and sea inspired me to see the whole world. (At present, I've seen the art in 26 countries). The beauty of the tropics

Petting a boa constrictor in the lobby of the Bel Mar Hotel.

also stirred a deep desire to paint.

The day after we returned from Mexico, I started O. Henry Junior High School. It was 1956 and school went well. I signed up for Latin and Spanish, as I planned to be ready for future travels. Life settled back to normal and I began painting as usual. I finished a work in casein entitled "Grief," which had a group of female faces with swirling veils around their heads, similar to the shawls the Mexican women wore. These connected to make a composition and were of different values of grey. The faces were colored in pale tints of pastels, mixed with pale grey. Even though it was a somber subject, the faces, the swirls, and the soft colors were peaceful and calm.

When it was finished, I had placed it on the dining table to dry as my mother's ladyfriend arrived for a visit. They had been talking for some time, when my mom called for me. The woman wanted to know all about my painting. After I finished explaining, she asked, "How much is it?" Wow! I was only 14 years old and in shock! I certainly had no idea about art prices! Finally I blurted out "fifty dollars," which was an extremely high price (equivalent to maybe $300 to $400 today). Even though it was an impossible amount, she beamed and said, "I'll take it." She actually wrote a check in my name! I was in a daze!

It turned out that she had recently lost her husband and was struggling with grief, so my peaceful, calm painting had spoken to her heart. That was a great lesson for me. Not only had my first sale catapulted me into the world of a professional artist, but it showed me that I should paint what I feel is right and the future will take care of itself. Paint what your heart tells you to paint. Don't worry about other's opinions, follow your inner guidance. There was also another lesson for me: I needed to open a bank account. The knowledge that I could make money as an artist was utterly thrilling!

A few months later, Lew and I got the shock of our lives. Our parents announced that they were getting a divorce. We were in disbelief. How could this be? Maybe my "Grief" painting was a premonition of things to come? Who knows? But, my childish joy disappeared and I felt so lost that my feet did not seem to touch the ground. I distinctly remember the odd feeling of floating through life, disconnected from the reality of gravity. Not many families divorced in those days, and I remember feeling shame. My self esteem plummeted and I retreated into my art. I was still in the UT Junior Art Project and my painting titled, "Underwater Swimmer" was chosen to be exhibited in their big Children's Exhibition, my very first Jury Show. This was great and raised my spirits a bit.

But, I still felt lost. For the first time in my life, I understood the meaning of tragedy. To my parent's credit, they worked out a very civil and fair arrangement, which kept Lew and me in our home and in the same schools. Mom stayed in the house for two weeks and then dad came for two weeks. They took turns, and with grandmother and grandfather next door, we children managed fairly well. It was relatively peaceful and stable for us. Thus, that became what I believed divorce was: a civil separation which protected the children and spared them as much grief as possible.

Three years passed and things became basically normal again. Then, my parents announced that they were getting remarried—to each other! And, they wanted Lew and me to go with them on their second honeymoon to Acapulco, Mexico.

Wham! A whole new set of adjustments presented themselves.

Mom and dad's first Acapulco honeymoon.

We were both teenagers and that stage is hard enough to traverse, without being compounded with additional family drama. In spite of my fears, we all went to Acapulco and managed to have a good time. The family reunited and my mom and dad ended up being married for 75 years! So "all's well that ends well." We were all very lucky that things worked out for the best.

I'm sure that other families thought our family was a bit odd, not only because of the divorce and re-marriage, but because we never had a television in our house. When TV became popular, my mom refused to allow one in the house. She called it, "the opiate of the masses," which, of course, devastated my brother and me. But, that horrible decree later proved to be quite beneficial. By the time I was 13, I had read world history, world religions, philosophy (good old Socrates), and copious amounts of good literature. This made high school and college relatively easy.

My boundless curiosity kept me really busy, and I drew so much that Mother could not keep enough paper in the house. To keep up with the demand, she became a paper "recycler" long before anyone had heard the word. Looking back on that, I have to laugh.

Instead of sitting in front of a TV, we were out swimming, water skiing, hiking, horseback riding, rollerskating, biking, even spelunking! Not watching endless hours of TV gave me time to paint for long periods. In high school, after I finished my homework, I would put on my favorite music and paint into the night. I remember my mom's amazement one morning, when she came in to wake me and discovered that I had completed five paintings overnight! That is the passion—the obsession—of a true artist.

Now, seeing the young people of today, with all their gadgets and electronic devices, I can see the enormous contrast between my active childhood and theirs. Not much is left to the imagination today. I believe that our imaginations are vital because they are our problem solvers, and we should be cultivating them, not replacing them with artificial activities. Life is precious and time is the most important thing we have, so I don't waste it. During this period, I read a biography of Benjamin Franklin, and one of his quotes struck me to my core: "Up sluggard and waste not life, in the grave will be sleeping enough." The power of this statement shook me then, and has propelled me forward all my life.

In 1956, I entered S. F. Austin High School. I had a car, my driver's license, and a group of seven girlfriends to run around with: Nonie, Cherry, Jacque, Sandra, Diane, Dinah, and Natalie. We finally had the freedom to explore our world. Every weekend we would all pile into someone's car and go to the lakes, the rivers, or to surrounding cities. Life was great—and fun! I was getting kudos in art class and was elected president of the Paint and Palette Art Club. I also did illustrations for the school newspaper and had many other school activities.

Two serious paintings got accepted into The Laguna Gloria Art Museum and the Wellesley Junior Art Exhibition. So I finally saw my work hanging in two museums! Soon, I would be heading to college and I felt very well-equipped, with good drawing and painting skills, art work that had already been accepted into museums, and a proven work ethic. I was very excited and proud.

I was beginning to build a large body of work, and both mom and dad helped me with the framing. They were always supportive of my art and helped me realize my dreams. Sometimes we found old frames that dad would cut to fit, or he would build frames. This was eventually getting out of control, so mom and I went to a gallery frame shop, which I think was called The Country Store. We went in almost weekly and eventually we became friends with the owner. He could see that, even though I was a teenager, I was serious, and he seemed impressed with my work.

Finally, one day he offered to handle my work! That was unexpected! I thanked him and politely said no, and then never mentioned it again. I really don't know why that was my response. I wish I had said, "I'll think it over." Now, years later, I really regret that I didn't "seize the day." I've often wondered how my life would have turned out if I had said yes. I wish mom would have at least discussed it with me. She had respectfully kept herself out of my business, which I appreciated, but I missed an opportunity that could have been pivotal.

Sometimes, when opportunities come out of the blue, be open to them. Don't say "no," say "yes," and at least see what happens. You can always say no later. Life is full of mini-miracles!

I started college in 1960 at the University of Texas in Austin. I majored in Fine Art, (Studio), with a minor in Art History. I had grown up in Austin, so I lived at home.

The University of Texas was enormous, with about 26,000 students. That was overwhelming, so I decided to pledge a sorority, Alpha Gamma Delta. It was good to have a "home away from home" and a new group of friends. It made college easier because of the support system that helped with scholastics, as well as social life. I was chosen as the sorority's art supervisor for three years. That was a lot of work!

College was a whirlwind of activity and successes. My life drawings were chosen by my professors to hang in the halls of the art department. Three paintings were exhibited at the UT Student's Exhibition. At age 19, I had my first one-woman show at the Ford Paint Company, twenty-five works entitled "Black and White." As a result, I was interviewed by KASE and KTBC radio.

At the age of 20, I had my second solo show at my sorority, with my photo on the cover of the sorority's national magazine. At 21, I had two shows, one at The Villa Capri, and one at The 40 Acres Club for the UT faculty. All this led to a 20-minute television interview at KLRN TV. My art career was starting to get real publicity and recognition. There were also numerous newspaper articles. That same year, I won three citations in the Campus Art Competition, which was juried by the UT art professors. Things were going better than I had ever dreamed. I was on my way!

Then in October, 1963, I met Joseph Parker Witherspoon lll, who had graduated from Princeton and was studying at the UT law school. We fell madly in love, were engaged in November, and married on December 21st during the Christmas holidays. A true whirlwind romance.

People say that "you will know your true love when they arrive." Both of us knew that this was "it." There was no question that we were destined to be together. I quit school, and got a job at the Texas Capitol to help put Joe through law school. In November, 1963, President Kennedy was killed and Texas Governor Connally was seriously injured. At that time, I was working in the office directly below the Governor's office, so it was extremely traumatic for us in the capitol. We heard screams and cries all over the building. Those were very shocking and tragic times for our country, and they came very close to home. After the ordeal, I saw the Governor many times in my office, still wearing bandages and his arm in a sling. He was injured much more seriously than people knew.

Shortly after our wedding, another tragedy struck. My beloved, sweet grandmother, Wilma D. Valentine, passed away. She was the light of my childhood and her unconditional love and caring contributed to my development as a person, as an artist, and as a spiritual being. She has always had a special place in my heart all my life. I still miss her.

Joe and I were very happy, and we both worked hard. When Joe's dad was asked to teach at Boston College (he was a professor of jurisprudence at the UT law school), we moved into their big home to caretake the property. This was a great financial help for us as newly weds, and much appreciated. Finally, Joe graduated, passed the bar exam and we were off to Houston. He had gotten his first job at Assistant District Attorney for Harris County, Texas. We were ecstatic.

We settled in, but Houston became really lonely for me. I had

Clockwise from top left: A junior at UT; Article about my first one-woman show, in the Austin American Statesman newspaper; Mr. and Mrs. Joseph Parker Witherspoon III (1970).

left my family, my university, my friends, and my burgeoning art career. We had only one car, which Joe needed for work at the courthouse downtown, so I was completely isolated. I plunged myself into decorating our apartment and being a good housewife, but I felt lost. Before we left Austin, we had planned to have our first baby, and now that Joe's career was established, we discovered that I was indeed pregnant. It was perfect timing because I was free to devote myself to motherhood. Our precious baby girl, Kelly Valentine Witherspoon, was born on October 11, 1965. She was perfect and beautiful, and had bright red hair. We were overcome with joy! What a blessed gift in our lives.

Kelly was my adorable little buddy. I loved being a mother and wanted to be the best that I could be. I read Dr. Spock's *Child Care* book, and everything else on childcare that I could find. My family was back in Austin, so I was on my own. Motherhood was utterly fascinating to me. Watching and helping a baby develop was the most important thing I could possibly do in life. I readily gave up painting to be a mommy, my greatest joy.

Kelly was a precocious child and was talking like a four-year-old when she was only two. I could see that she was really bored and under-stimulated, so I started looking for nursery schools. I discovered that the University of Houston had the best preschool in the city, so that made it possible for me to go back to school, too. This was exactly the stimulation we both needed. On her first day, she literally jumped out of my arms when she saw the kids. Our schedule was crazy. We drove with Joe to work, and then headed to The University of Houston nursery school, dropped off Kelly, then I went to classes until noon, picked up Kelly, headed home for lunch and her nap, and then back downtown to pick up Joe at five o'clock, and then back home for dinner. It was very demanding, but she and I thrived. I was still majoring in art, and studying at night after she was in bed.

When Kelly was three, I could see that she was ready to learn to read, so I bought a first grade reading book and began. She completed the book at three years old and Joe and I were so proud of her. The nursery school had been a great idea. I really believe in preschool for children and this experience proved it. I also believe in 'Mommy Education," too. I was painting again and loving it.

We reconnected with our Houston cousins, James and Martha Davis, and Liz and Rod Kelley, and their families. We also developed a wonderful friendship with Ann and John Heyburn and their family. Ann was a scholar, a writer, an art lover, and very spiritual, so we enjoyed a deep friendship while we raised our kids together. During this period, our intellectual conversations went on for hours, while the kids played. I was accepted into the Ann Morehead Gallery in Houston, and I was thrilled. My work was finally being exhibited again.

Joe worked for the District Attorney's office for three years. He did well, but it was his turn to feel that he was ready for more. He interviewed with the U.S. Attorney's office and got the job. The only drawback was that we had to move to Tyler, Texas. We were about half packed when we got a surprise. John Heyburn, Ann's husband, asked Joe to join his outstanding law firm, Strong and Heyburn. We rejoiced. It was a great move-up for Joe's career, and it meant we could stay. Kelly and I could continue at UH, and it was a great opportunity for our family.

At this point, Joe and I wanted our second baby, hopefully a boy. I stayed in my classes at the university until, very pregnant, I was feeling minor labor pains, and my professors were getting really nervous. Then, right on schedule, May 9, 1969, Adam Joseph Witherspoon arrived, our beautiful, healthy boy. We were blessed beyond words! We were utterly thrilled at his arrival, but we discovered that we needed another nursery. That meant we had outgrown our two bedroom apartment. It was time to buy our first house, and I wanted space for a studio. I hadn't had a place to paint for six years.

We found a cute three bedroom, with a screened in porch and a large backyard on Floyd Street in the Heights, which was only three blocks from Memorial Park. It was also much closer to town and Joe's work. Kelly, who had turned five, entered the Awty School, which she loved. It was a private school, kindergarten through six grade, and she excelled.

This enabled me to devote my time to Adam, which I loved. He was a happy-natured blond and loved to snuggle. He was also precocious and loved to play. With Kelly in school, Adam got as much attention as an only child, and I was thrilled to be able to focus fully on him. I taught him to read early, too. I was so lucky that I didn't have to hold a job. I could be a full-time mom. The four of us were healthy, growing, thriving and happy.

Joe did well at Strong and Heyburn. He learned a lot about private practice and he enjoyed it. His father and brother were both practicing law in Austin. I think that was his draw to move to Austin and open his own law firm. I was also concerned that our children were growing up without ever knowing their grandparents, a huge worry for me, since my own grandmother in Austin had meant so much to me. My mom heard about a house that was for sale; we checked it out and it was a great buy, plus it had enough room for all of our needs. We hated leaving our wonderful relatives and friends in Houston, but it was time for Joe to be his own boss. I could go back to school at the University of Texas and finish my degree, and the kids could finally have grandparents. Plus, my mom and dad owned a beautiful property 31 miles west of Austin. It was 25 acres in the Hill Country, with the Pedernales River on one boundary and crystal-clear Roy Creek running through it. This creek had a 17-foot-deep, natural swimming pool with waterfalls. We called it "Camp." We had missed going to Camp regularly for seven years. It was time to enjoy "Adam's Eden," Camp's official name, at last.

Our families were so excited to hear the news. The move wasn't so bad, and we settled on Everglade Drive in South Austin. Kelly went to Sunset Valley Elementary and Adam was old enough for Montessori School.

This was the first time I had been free of childcare since 1965, for

A natural swimming pool on our property, called Camp, 25 acres west of Austin.

eight years, so I planned to go back to college at age 30. Age didn't matter to me because I was determined to get my art degree, something that Joe supported, too. Back in 1963, when we had decided to marry, Joe had promised that if I put him through law school, he would send me to Europe to study art. That way, we could each help the other to make our dreams come true. I had heard about a UT art history course in Europe, taught by Dr. MacDonald Smith, Phd., a famous expert on the Renaissance. In six weeks of study, it would cover the Renaissance from Italy to England.

I was eager to go, and deliriously happy when Joe consented! We started saving money for this expensive trip, as tuition was $2,000. I couldn't believe it was going to finally happen. Then came a very big surprise. . . we were expecting our third baby! Of course, we were happy; but it appeared that I would miss my dream. I hoped that maybe Dr. Smith would take another trip again in the future?

I said a prayer.

I had kept my OB/GYN Doctor in Houston, who had delivered Adam, and I trusted him completely. As we drove to the appointment. I felt great trepidation because of a new serious problem. The birth control device, the IUD, was still inside my womb *with* my baby! Was my baby in danger? Could this hurt my baby's development? I was extremely upset. Also, the IUD was so new that my Austin doctors didn't really know what would happen. I couldn't get any real information and I was in a total panic! Fortunately, my Houston doctor had years of experience as director of a women's clinic. He said that since I had delivered two healthy babies, he expected that this one would be healthy, too. What a relief! I broke down and cried.

As the pregnancy progressed, I finally got the courage to ask him if it were safe for me to travel to Europe? He thoroughly checked everything and gave me the okay. I joyfully packed my bag. Mommy, *and baby*, were going to Paris to see the Louvre, at last! Hooray!

The itinerary was extensive. We visited every major art museum, every major church, every major sculpture, every important art work, and every major site in 9 countries. We saw art in the Netherlands (Holland), Belgium, Italy, Switzerland, Austria, Germany, France, Luxembourg, and even Liechtenstein, the smallest country in Europe. It was much more than my dream come true, because it was more vast and magnificent than anything I had ever imagined. It exponentially expanded and elevated my entire concept of art.

We moved fast, because we had to, there was so much to see and learn. We started in early morning and ended late at night. Professor Smith was like an encyclopedia, his knowledge was utterly amazing! I saw how movements like the Renaissance travelled north over the centuries and how art made history, and history influenced art. I realized how vitally important art is to the development of a civilization and its culture. I wished more Americans could see the value of art that the Europeans know and understand. The arts are the measure of a culture's worth and its achievements. I was both humbled and inspired by this extraordinary privilege and I felt the deepest gratitude to Joe and Dr. Smith for such a gift.

It changed my life and my career standards in the most profound ways. And my darling baby never gave me the slightest problem.

When I returned, instead of being exhausted, I was in the best shape I'd been in years. The miles of walking and climbing stairs had built me up physically, and the amazing sights had stimulated me emotionally and intellectually. I was so happy and excited I could hardly wait to see my tiny, precious traveling "companion." She came on September 17,1973 in Houston, Texas and we named her Alethea Katherine Witherspoon. Alethea is the Greek word for Truth, and I thought it was as beautiful as she was. Her hair was the color of honey and she had big blue eyes. All our children have beautiful blue eyes like Joe's. Alethea, being the third child, was nothing but joy!

Her needs were always met because her parents knew how to anticipate those needs. The third baby is much easier and everyone is more relaxed. Kelly decided that "Ali," Alethea's nickname, was *her* baby, and she would carry her around the house for hours. She was eight, and so she had a real, live baby doll to play with and love. We were so happy with our little family, with everyone so healthy and bright. I had my hands full and I loved it! There is nothing as rewarding as raising a family!

We had lived on Everglade Dr. for some time when disaster struck. A massive tornado hit South Austin and destroyed our roof, uprooted a big tree in our back yard and ruined our cars. After it passed, when we were able to call Joe at his office downtown, he had no idea what had happened. The four of us had been in real danger! It had come without warning and the shock had left the children and me feeling traumatized.

The day the roofers came turned into the most horrible day of my life. I was at home monitoring the roofing job, the kids were bored, and asked to go for ice cream. I gave permission, only if the 12 year old neighbor boy would go, plus Kelly was 11, so I felt Adam, seven, would be fine. As the roofers banged on the roof and I was folding clothes, suddenly, there was frantic banging on our front door. It was Paul, our neighbor screaming, "Kelly and Adam have been hit by a car, Hurry! Get in my car!" I grabbed Ali and ran to Susie's house across the street, and thrust her into her arms. Paul said an old lady's brakes had failed and she had hit them near the curb. There on the grass were my two babies covered with blood! Kelly was screaming and Adam was pale and moaning. I could see his thigh had been crushed and her leg was bent in the wrong direction. Oh my God! My God! Paul went to call EMS. I grabbed both their hands and tried desperately to comfort them. As I silently prayed, I was trying to send all my own life force into them through my hands. I wanted to "push" my life energy into them to save them. It was purely a maternal "instinct."

When the ambulance arrived, the EMS men ran straight to Adam, instead of Kelly, who was sobbing and screaming. I suddenly realized that it was Adam who was in the most danger. I shivered in fear! My God! All I could do was to keep telling them they would be okay. Joe was already at the hospital when we arrived. While they were working on Adam in the ER, the Doctor told me to go with Kelly to X-ray. He later confessed that he was trying to get me out of the room because Adam was in deep shock and he wasn't sure he would make it. Adam was in the ER for 5 hours, then into intensive care for 3 days. I didn't leave the hospital, sleeping on the floor, until he was out of intensive care. Both children had broken femurs and they were put into spika body casts, which ran from their armpits, down both legs, with a pipe between, spreading their legs. Pins were drilled into their shinbones to secure the position of their legs.

It was a horrific nightmare, and thank God our kids were strong and Alive! I was so proud of how incredibly brave they both were. When they were released, their casts were so heavy that it took two people to carry them, like pieces of furniture. They needed constant care, needing to be turned every 15 minutes to prevent bedsores. We hired a home care nurse because it was too much for one person. I was amazed at how they held up. They rarely complained, our amazing little troopers!

Thus began a year of body casts, bedpans, hand feeding, sponge baths, getting casts sawed off, wheel chairs, crutches and home schooling. Both kids had to keep up with their lessons, so I was their teacher for both grades. Amazingly, they did it!

Plus, darling Ali needed care, too. She was a toddler, but she didn't get my undivided attention until they were finally in school. Fortunately, Ali has always had a strong and stable personality. When things were overwhelming, she would take my face in her hands and tell me that things were going to be all right. That little "bundle of love" kept me going. She was my joy through it all.

Finally, the nightmare ended. They bounced back physically, but the trauma lingered for us all. Adam seemed to be the most effected. Our little family was never the same. I couldn't seem to get over the fear of losing a child. It haunted me. I had lost 17 pounds. I believe I, too, was still in shock. It had gone on so long. I'm sure that Joe was affected, but he had his office to go to and he seemed to fare better than we did, maybe because he was not at the scene of the accident.

I was never quite the same.

We finally decided to move, in hopes of putting everything behind us. One day, at lunch with my cousin, Julie Valentine, we happened to see a "For Sale" sign in front of a classic Spanish-style mansion on Windsor Road. It was in the neighborhood where I grew up. Out of sheer curiosity, we decided to look. It was beige stucco, with a red tile roof, and huge oaks. The living room was 40' long and 27' tall, with hand-painted one-foot beams. The walls were 3 feet thick. The doors had eight different archways. It was so unique that I called Joe to come look. I never thought it would become "The Villa de Zilla," which our friends jokingly named it. It had a solarium which was perfect for a studio, a library/office for a guest room, a breakfast and dining room, and a music room for all of Joe's instruments, he played guitar, mandolin, banjo, violin, and piano. We discovered that it was also the right price!

We all started a new life, three blocks from where I grew up on Parkway. Plus, the University, our alma mater, was about 7 minutes away. I felt I had finally come home.

It was 1977 and I had turned 35. The children's accident was over, but it had been a serious confrontation with death, and that often causes one to be confronted with one's own mortality. I be-

Left to right: The Villa de Zilla in Austin; in my living room; looking at drawings in my solarium studio; After the divorce, I moved to a smaller house of my own. My sculptures of a male and female nude were, unfortunately, stolen

lieve this pushed me into my "Mid-life Crisis" which was a new concept then, and there were no tools available to cope with it. Plus, the whole decade of the 1970's was already extremely unsettling for women.

Women had no preparation for the myriad challenges. Women's Liberation turned all of our roles upside down. Marriages were ending everywhere. I decided to plunge back into school. Maybe it and art would restore my soul? I worked hard and my drawing, "Zilla's House" was chosen to hang in the art department building, along with a painting entitled, "Frost." My etching, "The Cry" was juried by John Canady, the famous *New York Times* art critic. Two paintings, "The Genius" and "When All Else Fails" were shown in The Hunting Gallery of the art museum. I was finally successful again. That same year, Bill Wyman and Tommy Dale Palmore, both my art professors, invited me and Joe on an art trip to New York City. We visited 60 galleries and 5 major art museums in five days! It was grueling, but thrilling to me. In SoHo, I showed the manager of Hansen Gallery slides of my work, and he requested to see more. I was ecstatic, but this turned out to be Joe's and my last trip together. When we returned home, the divorce began. Unfortunately, this great opportunity was foiled by our marital problems.

At that point, I was rushing to finish my degree so I could support my children, if necessary. At 36 years old, I graduated in December 1978, after Joe and I had already separated. I had my Bachelor's Degree! It had taken me 19 years, but I did it!

The divorce took nine months and during that time, I was asked by Linda Schele, the famous Mayan scholar, who deciphered the Mayan language, to become her artist at her archeological dig site at Palenque, Chiapas, Mexico and Guatamala. She was so impressed by my drawings of the Mayan glyphs, she had my term paper put into the UT Latin American library and the library of the University of South Alabama. She sent me the job application and all the information, but I had to decline because the divorce was pending and I couldn't leave the country. Another missed opportunity due to marriage difficulties.

Months earlier, when we first began marriage counseling, our counselor had suggested a separation so that we could have time and space to work things out. Originally, Joe had agreed to get an apartment and he checked prices, which were around $700. This was a huge stretch for our budget. Coincidentally, my mom and dad left for an extended vacation to visit Lew in California, and they would be gone for months. So, I suggested to Joe that if I stayed at their home temporarily, it would cost nothing and we could achieve the same result.

It seemed to me to be the logical solution. Win, win. Unfortu-

nately, not so! I had no idea of the legal ramifications and consequences of being the person who "left" in a divorce. I was simply trying to follow our counselor's recommendations. Besides, the children would know I was at Granny's and Grandaddy's, which would seem normal, not a big deal. When I called Mom and Dad for permission, they unexpectedly rushed home to their daughter, which missed the point of having peace and time to work things out. I ended up moving into my studio on Sixth Street with no shower, nor private bathroom.

This is where my diamond wedding rings were stolen from my studio. The police thought they knew who did it, but I let it go. I dropped the issue. My mom, who feared that I was in a dangerous place, called the UT Student Housing Department, and since I was in school, I moved into UT's old World War II military barracks, which served as student housing. It cost $67.00 per month and the toilet froze at night. At least, I was able to finish my last semester and graduate.

Through out this whole period, I still picked the children up from school, took them to their after school activities, helped with homework, fed them dinner and took them home. I just did not sleep at their house anymore.

After I graduated, I was utterly displaced. No more student housing. The divorce was granted and the rest is history. Joe sold the house and moved with the children to Houston. Eventually Joe married a woman named Charlotte. And, that was that! I was completely heartbroken over the children being so far away.

I had lost everything that I ever loved, ever cared about, ever worked for, or ever wanted because of Women's Liberation and the Sexual Revolution of the 1970's. It had caused the breakdown of monogamy and marital commitments in our society, even to the point of the popular "trend" of couples practicing "wife swapping," all of which were disgusting to me! At least, now, I didn't have to deal with that nonsense any more.

I had lost the battle, but refused to be vanquished. After 16 years of marriage, I was back to Ground Zero. The world had changed during those 16 years. As a newly single woman, I found myself in completely unfamiliar territory. I just wanted peace and a job.

My old professor and dear friend, MacDonald Smith, called and said he wanted to help. He knew of a job at the University and he would recommend me. Bless his heart! I was hired as the Director of the UT Graphic Design Lab, doing commercial art, book design, museum catalogs, and publicity for the Art, Music, Drama and Dance Departments. My only problem was that I hadn't worked in graphics for 16 years, so I had to re-learn the entire subject before I showed up for work. I went to the UT book store, bought as many books on Graphic Design as I could carry, and read them all before

I arrived eight days later! Whew! Fear is a prime motivator. I never confessed this to "Mac," because my work proved to be very successful. I even designed museum catalogs for some of my former professor's shows, thus giving back to them what they had given to me. In eight months, I had built a professional portfolio worthy of a job at *Texas Monthly* magazine in the production department. Thus began my ten year career as a graphic designer.

Eventually, my children began to visit me in Austin. I had rented a cute two bedroom house, with a glass-enclosed studio on Oakmont Blvd. The kids had a room of their own, so they began to spend time with me in the summers, too. I had missed them terribly! I was now a working mom, but I only worked at *Texas Monthly* for two weeks per month (after the editorial department worked the first 2 weeks). So I was able to freelance for the remaining two weeks. This gave me free time to be with my children, at last. We were all finally getting somewhat adjusted to the dramatic changes. I was well aware of the children's struggles, but didn't have the money, nor the power to alleviate them. This was a pain and guilt that I've lived with for years. I had never dreamed that our divorce would have caused such a separation. That was my own naiveté and error in underestimating the situation. My children and I paid dearly for my lack of judgment and my ignorance of the legal system. I felt I had done the best I could, under the circumstances, but my best simply was not enough! Nor, would it ever be! Sometimes life deals us a situation that we can't remedy, no matter what. That doesn't mean that we dismiss it, the pain is always there.

I loved working at *Texas Monthly*! The people were creative, talented and fun. I met Janice Ashford there, a gifted designer, who became my best friend. She invited me to join her Sagebrush Studio group, with five top graphic designers and illustrators, who rented a large Victorian house on Sixth Street in Austin for their offices. I was honored to be with Tom Curry, Roberta Hill, Ellen Simmons, and Janice in a freelance environment. They were the best, and we had so much fun. We worked hard, and often we would break for champagne at 4:00 p.m. I began to build an important clientele and was finally making a decent living, at long last! Janice was married to an architect named Gary and they introduced me to John Doonan, who was also an architect.

Actually, I had met John earlier, when he rented his van to me for my move into my studio. He became a supportive friend and we ran in the same circles. Eventually we began dating. John owned a sailboat on Lake Travis, and I fell in love with sailing and him. It was so quiet and peaceful to let the wind carry us across the water. John was a quiet and peaceful man, too, which was just what I needed. We shared our love for art, architecture, music, literature, sailing and fun. I had never lived alone, having left my father's house to move directly into my husband's house. So, I had never lived my own life and the adjustment was lonely and weird. John was always there to help me, which I appreciated so much.

I also enjoyed work in the business world, because working only 8 to10 hours a day was a breeze for a mother who had worked 14 to 16 hours regularly, especially during my UT studies. In those days, I often put in18 hours as a student and a mother of three. John had been a bachelor all his life, so he really enjoyed my kids. We often went sailing together and the kids loved it. It was a great de-stressor for all of us.

He and I had a sometimes stormy, on again, off again, relationship. I was still very shell shocked from the divorce and I was guarded, afraid of being hurt. I was not very trusting and I was scared of commitment. Being a bachelor also kept him un- committed, so we got close and then bolted. It makes me laugh to recall those days and observe our commitment-phobic antics. That "ping-pong match" lasted four years before we finally got married.

John never talked much about his past, so it was after we got engaged that I heard about Evelyn. Actually, John had lived a fascinating life. His birth mother had contracted tuberculosis when he was an infant, so she gave John to her best friend, Evelyn, to care for him. Evelyn was childless and was a Countess, who had married a Spanish Earl who lived in Cuba. The Earl de Bario had passed away and Evelyn had moved back to the USA.

John eventually grew up with Evelyn and her second husband,

Joseph O. Lambert, a distinguished landscape architect from Dallas. John had traveled the world and had every advantage. Countess Evelyn and Joe Lambert had bought a massive villa in Vicenza, Italy, and along with the Italian government and the architect, Francesco Gnecci Rusconii, had restored this national treasure. It was designed by the famous Italian architect, Palladio. This is where Countess Evelyn lived when she heard that we were engaged. John hadn't told me any of these details, until our engagement, so I was surprised, to say the least!

Evelyn flew to Dallas to meet me, then on to Austin to meet Kelly, Adam and Alethea at the new house I had bought on Rosedale Avenue. She was an amazing woman, utterly gracious and cultured, and in love with life. The room lit up when she entered. She loved art and was an avid collector, so she and I immediately bonded over art. She announced that her wedding present to us was a honeymoon in Europe for the Christmas Holidays of 1981! I was astounded!

I married John Henry Doonan at my grandmother's home in Austin.

We were in Europe for a month on a whirlwind "grand tour." We landed in London in heavy snow, and she brought a full-length mink coat to keep me warm. This act was typical of her kindness and generosity to everyone. Our adventures would fill a book and I kept a detailed journal and photos of this glorious trip. First stop was the Spaghetti Boutique, owned by Nadia La Valle, the *Vogue* fashion designer and we met her 13 year old son, Sheik Karim Takkedine, whose father owned a Swiss chocolate factory. Karim studied at Marlboro College. I soon found out that Countess Evelyn had been written up in *Vogue, Architectural Digest, Tattler* (English), and *Arbiter* (Italian) magazines! The next day we visited Sean Connery's flat at Lennox Gardens, and numerous art galleries: White Chapel, The Juda, and the Waddington, plus the Royal Academy. I had been to London before, but not like this.

When we returned to Nadia's, where John and I were staying, we met Nadia's husband, Soumi, who had arrived from Lebanon. He was a professional photographer and was writing a book.

Jolly old London was turning out to be very exotic. Everyday was a new adventure. We shopped at Harrod's, the famous 900 year old department store, which was decorated for Christmas, something not to be missed. At the theater, we saw a play about Prince Charles and Diana, which featured a replica of her wedding dress.

Evelyn's birthday party was on December 20th, and Michael Roberts, the fashion director of *Tattler* magazine, and Clyde Arrowsmith, the famous European photographer were in attendance. Afterwards, we went to visit Billy Keating's Gallery, whose fiancée, Angela, was the daughter of Lord Nevelle, the Equerry to Prince Phillip. Her mother, Lady Nevelle, was the Queen's best friend. The Countess introduced John and me to all her esteemed friends!

The next morning, we all dashed to Victoria Station, with trunks of clothes, to take the train to Dover, then catch the boat to Calais, France. The French train had lavish decor and went 120 miles per hour. We had a night and a day in Paris.

Andre Dunstetter, who spoke eight languages, picked us up in his tiny Mini Minor, so we had to hire another cab for the luggage. The Seine River was flooding and the traffic was terrible, so Andre resorted to driving on the sidewalks! I Immediately saw the advantages of having a little car in Europe. His house was on St. Germaine Boulevard and he had to abandon the car ten blocks away because of the blocked streets. Andre worked worldwide as

Clockwise from top left: Countess Evelyn Kelly Lambert and John; A Veronese fresco in the Villa Lambert at Longa di Schiavona; An aerial view of the villa; A view of the front entrance of the villa.

a translator for numerous royal houses and businesses. The next day we drove to the Paris suburbs to "TiTi" Hudson's house, who was now the Princess Von Furstenberg. Her house was off the Blois de Belongna and her husband was the Prince of Monaco, cousin to Prince Renier. She was the Exxon heiress, one of the wealthiest people in the world. The house was fabulous, filled with Picassos, Braques, Van Goghs, Fontanas, and Mayan stelas. In the basement there was a swimming pool, with a glass wall and gardens that sloped up and outside, so it appeared to be outside. It was an awe inspiring visit. Then we drove to Fouchon Market, the most famous gourmet grocerie, to buy provisions for our picnic on the train to Italy. They had invented truffle ice cream, which was the rage in England at the moment. Since Karim had joined us, it took three porters to get our 15 pieces of luggage on the train in Lyon Station.

We would be in Vicenza, Italy at 8:30 the next morning. John and I watched the beauty of the night journey through the Alps with the falling snow. It was spectacular. I was so eager to see Evelyn Kelly Lambert's famous Villa Lambert at Longa di Schiavona.

Pietro, the Villa's butler-manager, picked us up and we drove about 30 minutes, and entered through two huge iron gates in a giant wall, to be greeted by a massive, white Pyrenees dog named, Freddie. The Villa Lambert was huge, with white stucco and a grey tile roof. It had 62 rooms, a 16TH century farm house, and a beautiful lake with swans. We entered the main door into an enormous ballroom, filled with an astonishing collection of art. It was icy cold and I immediately put on ski pants and apres-ski fuzzy boots. I got a quick reminder of the temperatures that the historic Italians had weathered in their day. Only a few of the personal living areas were heated. Evelyn had been living in this remarkable masterpiece since 1970. She had worked with the designer, Robert Wedel, to install her magnificent contemporary art collection, which was breathtaking!

A partial list of the artists included Picasso, Dali, Calder, Jean Arp, and Rietveld's famous Red-Blue Chair. Jules Olitski, Enrico Castellani, Dorazio and Fontana were also featured, along with superb antiques and exotic collectibles, all beautifully arranged. Evelyn's taste was eclectic, expansive and very good! It was the most delightful 'museum' I had ever seen and a very personal expression of her lively personality.

The Villa was designed by the most famous Italian High Renaissance architect, Andrea Palladio, who is historically considered one of the most influential in all of Western architecture. He was born in 1508 and died in 1580 at 71 years old. His work was influenced by ancient Roman and Greek architecture. At age 16, he settled in the Veneto and Vicenza, where he gained fame for his villas and palazzi (palaces).

His works were aristocratic in style and emphasized an aesthetic quality, for those of high social position. He collaborated with the famous artist, Paolo Veronese, in creating illusionistic paintings and frescoes to decorate his buildings. He became the chief architect of the Republic of Venice. Famous buildings in America, which are in the Palladian style, are the National Gallery and the United States Capitol in Washington, DC. The fact that Evelyn and Joe Lambert decided to restore a Palladian Villa of 62 rooms is a testament to their extraordinary character, intellect and heart.

After our arrival, Andre, Evelyn, John and I went to visit one of Evelyn's dearest friends. We drove to meet with Dame Freya Stark, the British writer, in Asolo, a charming medieval city. Dame Freya's house overlooked a beautiful valley. She was 91 years old and was a world famous writer. The University of Texas had just bought her letters. During World War II, she had been characterized as the female version of Laurence of Arabia. The story was that she had persuaded the Arabs to support the Allies, or at least to remian neutral, which was pivotal to us winning the war. For this, she had been knighted by the Queen of England. She was also an early explorer of the Middle East. She explored Beirut, Iraq, and did three dangerous treks into the wilderness of Western Iraq. In Southern Arabia, she ventured farther than any Westerner had. She then wrote travel books about her adventures. She had just gotten back from a trek in the Himalayan Mountains in Tibet and a raft trip down the Euphrates River. Both of these expeditions had been filmed as documentaries.

She was a small women, with a sweet face, wearing an old fashioned black skull cap with lace around the edges. As a little girl, her hair had gotten caught in a weaving machine and it had partially scalped her. She suffered in the hospital for months getting skin graphs. To me, she was quaint and adorable. Of her most recent travels, she said: "Well, I've found that after 70, one cannot walk up the mountains any more, but one can ride an agreeable little pony indefinitely!" She was utterly charming and dear and we had tea.

She gave me one of her books, *A Peak in Darien*, which I still treasure. We bid her goodbye, "Addio" and walked to the Villa Duse, named for a famous Italian movie star, then to the Hotel Villa Cipriani, where Elizabeth Taylor and Richard Burton spent their honeymoon. Evelyn had lived there while her Villa was being restored.

Back at the Villa, every morning at 9:00, Pietro would bring us breakfast in bed on a silver tray, with fresh roses and silver teapots. To prepare for Christmas, everyone went to town to shop. At lunch, we talked about a book on Palladio that Evelyn was assisting in the publishing. The last printer was holding the etching plates, which were public domain, so an attorney was needed. At 3:30, we left to attend a Christmas party hosted by the Comte and Contessa Di Lord at their Villa in Asolo. The house was incredible and the Comte was dressed like Santa Claus, seated on a red brocade throne, handing out gifts to the children. They were adorably dressed in velvet and lace, even the boys had velvet shorts and lace collars. A choir of Alpini soldiers, who fight in the Alps, were dressed in white Swiss-style uniforms with Tyrolean hats with red feathers. Their songs were very mellow, but powerful. I wished with all my heart that I could speak Italian. Having studied Latin, Spanish and French, I had been able to understand enough, and I was picking up words really quickly, but these songs were so touching. It was a wonderful night.

On Christmas Eve, Nadia and Soumi had arrived to join Karim and us at the Villa. We arranged the gifts around the huge tree in the Grande Salone Ballroom. Dinner was at 9:00 in the fresci room, which has the 15th and 16th century frescoes. We ate by candlelight because, in centuries past, frescoes were to be seen only by candle light, and in the daytime, only by daylight coming in through the windows. Evelyn's dishes were designed in Basano di Grappa, the ceramic center, from a fragment she had found in the rubble during the renovation. They were signed with V L for Villa Lambert. It was enchanting to dine in this room with such elegant surroundings.

The most famous frescoes in the Villa Lambert are attributed to the Italian Renaissance painter, Paola Veronese, who was born in 1528 in Verona (his name came from his birth city), and who died in 1588 in Venice. His mother was the illegitimate daughter of the noble man, Paolo Caliari, so he used that name at times to sign his work. He collaborated with the architect, Palladio, on numerous projects, and his work can be found in other Palladian Villas. This honeymooon was turning into a lesson in art history.

On Christmas Day, we were to open presents at 10 a.m. Andre and Karim played Santa. Evelyn gave me a Venitian Comedia del Arte Theater mask from the 17th Century, which was now the oldest mask in my collection, numbering 145. I was utterly thrilled! We drank champagne and unwrapped presents until almost noon. We had to be dressed by 2 p.m. for the arrival of our guests for Christmas luncheon. Evelyn had planned a beautiful party for 52 guests. I wore my silver and turquoise Native American Indian squash blossom necklace and a Guatemalan huipil, a brightly colored, hand-embroidered tunic, both of which were very American. The noble guests began arriving, the *acculturati* of the Veneto and Vicenza in northeast Italy.

A little six year old girl dressed as Santa played the mandolin to begin the festivities. After her adorable performance, a choir of 30 members sang Italian carols, their voices filling the grande salone. Among the guests were several counts and countesses, barons and baronesses, princes and princessas. I sat next to Countess Evelyn and the Baron Dominico di Schio and the Baronesse. The food was delicious, the chef having been brought in from the Hotel Villa Chipriani. Evelyn made a presentation of golden rings to all of her godchildren and to me, her new "daughter-in-law." The rings had her silhouette engraved in the center, a gift that I still treasure.

Evelyn asked me to stand, and in the sweetest words, presented me to the group, saying that she was delighted than I had joined the family and that I was the newest asset to her family. All the glasses were raised and I felt truly deeply honored! We all got up and kissed Evelyn and the lunch began. Some of the guests included the family of Count Ceschi, the Princess Cristina of Portugal and Ambassador Franco of Italy.

As the meal was ending, a burst of sunlight hit the windows and we saw the most brilliant sunset. It had been grey for three days. We all jumped up from the tables and went out to the terrace. A blazing red and magenta light was illuminating the garden and lake that Joe Lambert had designed, and the tower across the lake, and the snow on the mountains. Everyone felt a blessed feeling of togetherness and the Contessina Chesci exclaimed, "It is a Christmas wish from God!" People said it was the first time anything like that had been witnessed, and we laughed and thanked Evelyn for arranging such a spectacle for us on Christmas Day! Slowly the guests graciously left and Evelyn opened more gifts. Karim put on music and we all danced until nearly collapsed. I was really tired, but we had to go and freshen up because we were invited to Count Ceschi's Villa in Vicenza for dinner.

Their Villa was perched high on a hill and was a fine house filled with antique Flemish and Italian paintings. We saw an engraving of the Count's family tree and Andre explained some of the histories of the Royal families, some going back to the Czar of Russia. It was here I met Katherine Donnally, who said she and her husband, who were sailors like John and I, had expatriated from California. That after seeing Europe, she had never felt the same about the USA, and decided to live in Italy. I said I had felt the same ever since my European travel in 1973. It had been a wonderful Christmas Day and on the way home, John whispered that he had married an incredible woman and that he loved me. Evidently, I had carried myself well all evening.

On Sunday, John wanted to go out to the lake and row the boat. The fountain had frozen over and had made the most gorgeous ice sculpture. The ice-covered trees looked like ice-spaghetti. From the boat, we threw ice chunks across the icy lake and they made the loveliest tinkling sound. Just then, the distant church bells rang and together, we made a winter ice symphony, which sounded like fairy music. It was magical. That afternoon, we visited the Thomas Marshalls. They had restored the Villa and farm house that was part of the Palladian Rotunda, the most famous of Palladio's designs. Thomas Jefferson had seen it and had designed Montecello after it. Tom Marshall was a concert pianist and all their children were musically gifted. Their kitchen dated from the 15th century, with a massive fireplace and hearth, and large polished copper pots hanging all around. We ate Italian chocolate cake with pudding inside and capuccino. On the way home, we passed another Palladian Villa. The whole area is a constant education in 15th and 16th-century art history.

In the library, I had found an Italian language book to study. For the next trip, I will study hard BEFORE I leave home. We took several side trips over the next few days, Morostica, Asiago, and in Vicenza, I got to see the Basilica di Palladio in the Piazza di Seniori, which I had studied 10 years earlier with Dr. Smith. It was the seat of local government and was full of remarkable frescoes.

On New Year's Eve, we were visited by Count Angelo Valmarana, who invited us to his Castle of the Dwarfs, as it is called in art history books. The outer walls have statues of dwarfs on top, thus the name. The castle has been in the Valmarana family for 900 years. We were to have tea and see the famous Tiepolo frescoes. The artist, Giovanni Battista Tiepolo was from Venice, born in 1696 and died in 1770. In the Republic of Venice, he was considered one of the greatest painters of the 18th century and one of the Old Masters of Europe. Veronese and Tintoretto were his predecessors. He was painter to the Doge Carnaro and was married to the sister of Giovani Guardi. He also worked for King Charles III of Spain on the Royal Palace in Madrid. His work in the Veneto spanned the years 1753 to 1770. Needless to say, I was thrilled to see this private collection. When the four of us arrived, the Count received us graciously and served us wine from his own vineyard. He was charming, and dressed in a tweed jacket with leather elbows and casual shoes similar to the "Hushpuppies" brand in the US. I thought this was adorable. The Tiepolo Fresci were in the Grande Salone, and

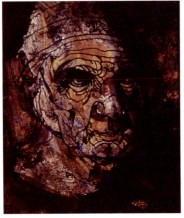

My two paintings: the Cathedral of San Marco in Venice, Italy, and the Doge who designed the look of Venice as it is today.

wonderful. There were also portraits of all the Valmarana Counts, down through history, displayed around the enormous room. That was very impressive and I vowed to do a genealogical search of my own family upon my return home. It must be wonderful to have that kind of knowledge of your ancestry and place in the world. What a rare treat to have tea in a castle with the lord of the manor. He was so kind to give us that privilege.

That night, we had dinner in Evelyn's fresci room, where the four walls are painted with "The Four Seasons" by artist, Pozzo Serrato, a Dutch artist, born in 1550, who had changed his name to be able to have a career in Italy. He was still living in 1604. In the candle light, the feeling was cozy, yet mysterious, as if we had somehow stepped into the past. This was a part of the Villa that the government won't allow anyone to disturb.

It is so valuable and revered. The Von Kassels were arriving from Venice to join us for New Year's Eve.

The party was at the Venable's home, which had Timothy Hennessee murals on the walls. Evelyn also had a large Hennessee wallhanging in her Grande Salone. It was a seated dinner for 100. After dinner, Kristen Venable passed out Venetian masks and noisemakers and the fun began. The orchestra from Venice had a wide repertoire and played everything from tangoes to the Beatles and nearly everyone danced for hours. Afterwards, we went to the Hotel Villa Cipriani for breakfast at 4:00 and got home at 5:00. It was the best New Year's celebration of my life. These Italians never sleep!

On New Year's Day, Evelyn, Andre and John and I ate bowls of black eyed peas for good luck, an old Southern tradition back home. At 4:00, we went to see Dame Freya again, one last time. At 91, she believes she is "in the transition" between life and death, and she has the most extraordinary *presence* about her. She commands a reverence from those around her that transcends the typical respect for elders. She is a philosopher and spiritualist, and we were all clinging to her every word. This was a profound and meaningful way to start the year 1982, and to end our days in Vicenza. I felt very privileged to be in such company.

Finally, on January 4th, we packed to go to Venice for one day and then leave for England the next day. After packing, Evelyn's plan was for John and me to plant two fir trees in Joe's Garden on a little hill at the corner of the property. One was for John and one for me. I was so completely touched by this beautiful gesture, and afterwards I felt truly as one of the family. It was a great honor to know Evelyn. We bid farewell to the Ceschis at tea, and ate our last dinner with Nadia and Soumi, Karim and Andre, all of whom had to leave early because of the fog.

On January 5th, Evelyn, John and I caught the train south to Venice. She told us the good news that Von Kassel was donating the money to publish the Palladio book. I know it made her happy to be able to contribute to the art history of Italy. We arrived in

Venice and boarded a vaporetto (a bus boat) and took a slow cruise down the Gran Canale. It was so beautiful to be back in my favorite city again. We passed the Palazzo Polignac, where Evelyn had lived, which was owned by the Duke and Duchess De Cazes. The Prince's wife had been Mrs. Singer, of the sewing machine fortune. When Prince Polignac was visiting the Palazzo Barbara (where we had drinks), he was so taken by the view that Mrs. Singer gave it to him for his birthday. Evelyn said that the grand nephew of the Prince had told her that story. We went to the Von Kassel's palazzo for lunch, then on to visit with the Baronessa Christina Franchetti, Evelyn's dear friend.

Venice is the world's most romantic city, so it was the perfect place to end our honeymoon. At 5 o'clock, we entered the magnificent Cathedral of San Marco to see the light of dusk hit the gold mosaic walls. We lit candles and said little prayers for all our loved ones, especially for my children. It was the perfect goodbye to Venice.

We caught the train back to Vicenza, where there was a dinner in our honor hosted by the Pievesan family. It was delicious, and jovial—but I felt a bit sad. The next day, we had our last lunch of spaghetti at the Villa Lambert, wrote thank you notes and "Love to Evelyn" in the Villa's big leather bound guest book. We took our last photos and said, "Addio." We all had tears in our eyes, even Pietro. John and I were headed to Milan and I was so deeply grateful to Evelyn for giving me the experience of a lifetime! It was like to most incredible dream. Unfortunately, I was never to see dearest Evelyn again.

Back in Austin, John's career really took off. He was working for John Lloyd, an architect and developer. I had gotten a job as production manager for two computer magazines, 26 miles away. I had sold my little Rosedale house and put the money into my new house on Bulian Lane in West Lake Hills. It had four bedrooms and a swimming pool, so the kids could come for longer periods and really have fun. Ali decided to move back to live with us. I was utterly thrilled! I was finally able to spend extended time with my youngest darling! She had her own room and started school in the Westlake district, which was noted for its quality education. All was going well between us, except I was now a working mom. We spent as much time together as possible.

John and I were working a lot. After our glorious trip with Evelyn, Texas seemed uninspiring, to say the least. After our honeymoon, John seemed to withdraw. Things were never the same.

After three years of marriage, it seemed like our relationship was fading into the mist. We didn't talk about anything really personal, just about what was going on at work. We didn't make plans, nor travel, nor was there ever any discussion of our future. John seemed preoccupied, or focused elsewhere. We had been together for seven years, so maybe that was it? I thought maybe he was depressed, or had met someone. Finally, I saw the writing on the wall, I just knew that the marriage had run its course. Oddly enough, I felt relieved. I finally told John I wanted a divorce, and I was expecting some kind of rebuttal or resistance, or maybe a rare declaration of love. He simply packed some belongings and left without comment. Eventually, we met at the attorney's office, signed the papers, and he walked me to my car. He quietly said, "I thought we were going to grow old together." Wow, who knew? He had never said a word. I drove away and never saw John again. Oddly enough I didn't feel sad. I felt closure. It was like watching an unspectacular sunset, as the sun silently drops out of sight and one simply turns and resumes one's day.

I had been married a total of 19 years, plus four years engaged, so a total of 23 years, and I was back to ground zero again. Plus, while our divorce was pending, my doctor found a lump in my breast. After the surgery, he had reported that it was a fibrocystic sarcoma tumor, cancerous, but that he had gotten it all. So... yet another negative issue to deal with. I got out of the hospital and reported back to work. The Editor, my boss, called me into his office, and fired me! Really! I had just won two Folio Awards in Graphic Design in New York for my work at his company and he had even kept one of my Awards to hang in his office! Unbelievable!! On the drive home, I started laughing. I had just gone through a divorce, cancer surgery, and getting fired! The Universe was certainly cutting me loose... to take another path?... but where? And for what?

The seven year cycle had ended with a bang. But, at least, I had Ali with me, so I was greeted by her beautiful face and her hug when I got home.

After the surgery, a woman I had met named Alegria, recommended that I go to a therapist named Alan Mesher, who did "energy therapies." I didn't really know what that was, but I was so exhausted from all the recent stresses, I agreed to go. I didn't know it at the time, but this would be a pivotal experience which would turn into a career path for me years later. During the same period, another "energy practitioner," who I had met at my former job, called me. Her name was Karen Wakeman and she also offered to give me a therapy with "light energy." Afterwards, I felt that my stress, fatigue, and any potential cancer had left my body. The power of both these experiences was utterly astounding and I vowed to explore them in the future. I felt totally "whole," at last.

I started freelancing again on two other magazines in my home office. But I had lost the drive to do graphics. I had done part-time commercial artwork in my twenties, beginning in 1962 and started my graphic design career in 1978. It was now 1983, so I had been at it for 21 years. Yet, I still needed to make enough money to support Ali, so I started real estate school with Keller-Williams Realty.

It was then that I got the chilling news that my insurance company refused to pay the $20,000 bill for my cancer surgery. They claimed that it was a pre-exisiting condition, which of course, was not true. I was in a panic! I had put every cent I had into my Bullion Lane house. With no full time job, no adequate savings, and no income

My daughter, Alethea, when she was living with me in Westlake Hills, near Austin.

yet from real estate, my only choice was to sell the house. This would totally wipe out all my work for the last six years and it exemplified the devastating power wielded by the insurance companies in those days. They could destroy a family with one sentence.

Ali had been living with me for some time and I didn't realize that our home sale would become that unsettling for her. I was madly trying to regain my strength and get a new career going, plus we were going to have to find a new place to live, which might mean a school change for her. I was trying my best to work it all out, but the future was very uncertain. Plus, Joe was remarried and settled, so Ali asked if she might go back to live with her dad. That made me very sad, but I understood how she felt. I finally realized that I couldn't provide for her in the manner she deserved. It was so hard to let her go, but if that was what she needed, then I understood. Children need stability, and my life was anything but stable. I love you, darling Ali!

I cried the whole day after she left. As a single parent, I had to face the fact that I couldn't support us financially, so I *had* to sell the house. I literally had no choice.

The sale took several months and I got a call from one of my graphics buddies, Robert. He said he had a friend who wanted to meet me. I was lonely, but I was busy starting a new life, so I felt conflicted. But, then I got curious, so I said yes. Terry Duff had been a friend of Robert's for years, so I felt it would be fine. Besides, it was Thanksgiving, so I welcomed some company. He was immediately interesting, lived on a sailboat in Kemah Marina on the Texas Gulf coast. He was a professional photographer with a degree from Brooks Institute of Photography in Santa Barbara, California. He was an accomplished guitarist and was also a freelancer. He had a 50-Ton Sea Captain's license and he loved ocean sailing. He was active, happy and seemed to love life and adventure. We hit it off immediately. He showed me that life could be fun again and I definitely needed that. We went sailing off shore on his boat, The Rebel, and it lifted my spirits. I am an innately happy person, so this was really a refreshing change. We had started dating, but I really did not want to get serious with anyone. I had responsibilities and I had my own plans in the works. But, after Ali left, I lost my drive to create a career, and have a home. I felt utterly defeated. Divorce, cancer, job loss and now the loss of Ali was the final straw. I just didn't care what happened. I had no idea what to do or where to go. With the sale of the house, I had no office to do my freelance work, so basically I was unemployed and homeless. Geez! But, I had survived such things before, so I believed I would survive again... somehow.

Terry had sort of a "Crocodile Dundee" aura about him. He was very masculine, and his sense of humor was so entertaining. Looking back, I think I had more in common with him than any other man in my life. We blended well in all aspects and our personalities and our philosophies were very similar. He was also an artist. Finally, Terry invited me to move onto his boat. I said, "no." I was focusing on selling my home. He asked me again, and I said, "no." He talked about sailing around the world and it sounded fabulous. I had always loved to travel. My home sale finally closed and I realized I had no place to go, so he asked me again and I said, "yes." By that time, we were falling in love.

It was 1984, I was 42 years old, and I had never had any freedom. At 21, I had married, leaving my father's house to join my husband. Thereafter, I was a wife and a full time mother of three, I was always in school, or had a job, or had a lease, or a mortgage, something that kept me committed or in one place. Suddenly, all of those ties had disappeared. I felt like I was floating. I had never experienced real freedom like this. It was weird, and scary, and exciting, and foreign, and liberating. A door had opened that had never opened before and I just decided to cast my fate to the four directions. At least, I had a partner who wanted to do the same, and who wanted to do it together. I moved my belongings into two giant storage

I moved onto Terry Duff's yacht, the Rebel, and we sailed from the Texas coast to Key West, Florida.

spaces, packed my boat clothes and gear and left my Volvo station wagon with my folks for them to use. We planned to go to the Bahamas and sail for three months and then I could come back and start my real estate career. Dad had told me he wanted me to sell his farm for him, so I took him and mom to meet Jim Williams at Keller Williams and Dad decided to list it with them. That would certainly launch my career in real estate.

I had lived in Austin from 1942 to 1964, and again from 1971 to 1985, a total of 35 years. It was my home and yet I felt that recent events seemed to be pushing me away from Austin. Maybe there were just too many sad memories there.

Terry had gone to art school on a scholarship and I had my fine art degree, so we both intended to get back into our painting. I had been a success in graphics, for which I had no official training, so I was sure I could make a success as a fine artist again. Plus, my living expenses on the boat would be low, which would also help the financial picture. I was so excited at the prospect of fulfilling my fine art dream again!

We made a list of all the preparations and Terry said I needed my scuba certification, so I started my scuba lessons in February in Lake Travis. Brrrr! I think Terry was definitely impressed that I was willing. He went with me, and both of us passed our Open Water Certifications in 53-degree water, in 43-degree weather, with 18-knot winds and whitecaps. The icy water literally "burned" any part of our skin that was exposed outside the wetsuit. I think this showed him that I was committed to our plans. I wasn't really afraid of the sailing, as much as, how the relationship would withstand living in a space 10' by 36' for months and enduring every kind of test. I just had to have faith that we could pull it off.

Since Terry had lived in California, he had been exposed to avant garde ideas and metaphysical subjects that I had never heard about, so we went to book stores together. I started reading *The Seth Material* by Jane Roberts, which was all about her channeling an ancient spirit, and describing the nonphysical world. I've always been determined to keep an open mind and I found it fascinating. I had already had so many mysterious occurrences in my life that I was open to new ideas. We were agreeing on reincarnation, and I said I felt that we were supposed to be together, as in our destiny. Terry agreed and said he thought I had been "sent" to him. We decided that we were "natural mates," as "in the order of things." I vowed to let myself trust again.

I had missed Ali so much, so I gathered her remaining belongings and went to Houston to deliver them. I got to see Adam, too, who I had missed for a year. He had turned 16. It was so hard to say, "goodbye," but I was actually moving closer to them.

On March 1, 1985, I moved onto Terry's boat, a 36-foot Pierson Yawl yacht, designed by the famous designer, Alberg. The next day was Texas Independence Day, so that seemed fitting. By April, I had already started painting again, very colorful, multidimensional abstracts. I felt so happy and creative and fulfilled.

Maybe this creativity had released something inside, because I started having amazing dreams that were very intriguing. I didn't know whether they were premonitions or memories of past lives, or what? In the first dream I had a river of energy flowing through me and a transparent white figure, a woman in a white gown, gave me a large green jeweled ring which seemed to be the key to some kind of powers. It was an emerald and cut with many gleaming facets. When I took it, I began feeling joy and a light was passing from her into me. I was glowing all over with the light of joy. Every molecule was charged with ecstasy that was unparalleled in physical existence, and as I awakened, these feelings carried over into reality. I could only describe it as "knowing a part of God." A few days later, I had another dream of being among Mayan temples and I was a healer, and healing the people for whom I felt an intense responsibility. In the third dream, a brilliant jewel came out of the darkness, it was huge, but not made out of anything physical. The facets were made of light. It was as if my spirit, not my eyes, were perceiving a symbol of pure knowledge and joy, and I was being given a spiritual message of who I really was. The fourth dream was about my grandmother, Wilma, being my spiritual "guide." Very intriguing, to say the least! I hoped I would come to understand the meanings, and eventually I did, years later. These dreams were pivotal to my life and my path.

On June 12, Kelly called from Venice, Italy. She was traveling on the Art History trip, which I had given her, with my dear old professor, MacDonald Smith. She was bubbling over with excitement, and thanked me a hundred times. She couldn't wait to tell me everything. I told her that I wanted all my three children to be "Citizens of the World." She said she hoped to study in Florence next year and MacDonald knew of a program. I was so thrilled to hear how her eyes had been opened.

I was wanting to give the same kind of gift to Adam and Ali, too. Terry and I discussed inviting our sons on our sail, and decided it would be great. He invited Patrick, 17, and I invited Adam, 16, so we had to wait until both boys were out of school. This would be late June, which would put the trip into hurricane season, but we felt we could risk it. I told Ali I would fly her to the Bahamas after we arrived and she would have a trip, too. But, she was very resistant. She was only 12, so maybe she felt too young. I felt sad, but I would try again later. Maybe she would change her mind? Meanwhile, I had painted eight paintings in eight weeks time, even in spite of the boat preparations, which were demanding.

There are whole books on preparing to go to sea. The chores are endless. We split the cost of a 12-foot Zodiac raft and a big out board motor. We pulled the boat out and into the boat yard for a bottom paint job. It was hard labor in 90-degree weather for 4 days. Other sailors joked: "We see that y'all are still speaking!" There had been times when we hadn't, during the long four months.

The departure date was fast approaching when a Marina neighbor, a lady named Taffy "rang" the boat's doorbell, which was rung by grabbing one of the stainless steel stays and plucking it hard like a harp. It sent a vibrating *Brong* through the whole boat. She had come to give me a woman-to-woman pep talk. She was full of suggestions to set my mind at ease. She cautioned me "to change out of wet clothes immediately to prevent getting sores like boils."

"And when the rain is coming, do all your wash so you will have a fresh water rinse." She said, " Men and teen age boys won't admit to being sea sick, so watch for lots of burps. Turn the eggs once per

Above: Terry's son, Patrick, age 17; below: my son Adam Witherspoon, age 16, on the crossing of the Gulf of Mexico.

week and they will last without refrigeration for six weeks."

I showed her my *Cruising Chef* book, which I had already read. She continued, "Zucchini and cabbage last forever and get Hormel canned ham, like tuna cans, because it tastes the best. And, have all kinds of candies, cookies, chips, snacks, and peanut butter individually wrapped to pep you up emotionally, and chocolate chip cookies are literally 'medicinal' when you are at sea." (I didn't realize that there would be times when it would be impossible to eat, because during storms, we would be fighting for our lives).

"Someone always has to be on watch, so your watches should be three hours: 9-12, 12-3, 3-6, with two people on and two people asleep. Then the second night, reverse it. And, always braid your hair because it can get caught in wires and lines. Wear safety harnesses during nasty weather and always after dark. And, keep them clamped to the boat at all times. Birds land at night. No matter what it costs here, it will be triple out of the country. If you say: 'I'll get it later or we'll do without,' shame on you! Buy more salad dressing, pickles, olives, because you always buy too much meat. Re-provision in, either Puerto Rico or the Virgin Islands, they are only a little bit higher. Don't leave the shower bag hanging and buy a barf bucket with a lid. Put a bay leaf in the corn meal and flour. Always have a line trailing out the back in case someone falls overboard, they can catch it. Avoid Andros Island and Norman's Key because they have pirates."

And, finally, she said, "There are a lot of fools out on the water and those are the ones who never say a prayer or two. Fear is natural, just don't panic." She said, "I would go in a minute if I could." She handed me an armload of wellworn Bahamian charts, and said, "It's the people you meet that makes it wonderful." I could say the very same about her, and the sailors I had already met.

They were a special breed. They were fun loving, independent, self sufficient, raucous, and sometimes ribald, but they would give you their last crust if you needed it. They were also addicted to nature and life, which has developed a spirituality in some. I have found their vitality and adventurousness both invigorating and inspiring. They would go out of their way to help you if you were in trouble. Remember, there is no ambulance, no doctor, no policeman, no fireman, no help of any kind out there. We are on our own in every regard, and are totally responsible for our fates, period. So, that's why sailors stick together and are so willing to help. They may need that same help themselves, one day. This was so amazing to me, coming from a city where help was just a call away. My admiration was to grow even more in the days to come. During our last days in Kemah, our sailor friends came with gifts: a scuba regulator, a glow in the dark emergency book, an extra safety harness, an extra log book, a Guide to the Intracoastal Waterways, a printout of all the addresses and numbers of the neighbors, plus new music tapes.

Charlie had an interesting comment: "There are two kinds of people who go to sea, those who go for fun and to meet people, and those who go to get away from everybody." I wondered which I was? Maybe both? Mother and Daddy had done so much to help me leave Austin, and Kelly came to say goodbye and bring Adam's passport. Dave and Linda organized a big farewell dinner at the Italian restaurant.

After three days of false starts, we actually cast off from the dock at 1:39 p.m. on Thursday, June 27, 1985, waving madly to Charlie, who was clicking photos from Pier 7. The weather looked ominous to starboard and it was pouring rain on High Island. We got into the Ship Channel and decided to motor-sail to keep away from the big barges and ocean liners. We were carrying $900 in provisions, and our only sons, out to sea in Texas hurricane season. I thought about Taffy's comment about sailors who pray and I said a long silent prayer. The wind changed and the storm retreated behind us. We had done it!

We arrived at Galveston and anchored to watch a beautiful sunset. As soon as it dropped, swarms of giant mosquitoes attacked. It was maddening as we jumped around wildly swatting in every direction. I had already bought the nylon mesh for screens for the hatches, but I just hadn't had time to sew them. Eventually, covering up under sheets in the heat, we dozed off about 3:00 a.m., when two of Terry's friends motored up to visit, 'if we were still awake."

Argh! We were awake now. We dozed off again around 5:30 and got up at 8:30. Exhausted, we looked like measles victims. Obviously, my first job was to make the screens ASAP. This was no way to start our voyage—with no sleep. I was to learn that no sleep was to be the norm, so get used to it.

I knew Terry was a very good sailor, who had sailed on a famous tall ship from California to New York for the Tall Ship Exhibition. He had considerable ocean sailing experience, so I had faith in his abilities. I also knew that sailboats are more sea worthy than motorboats because of the weight in their keel. When a sailboat is knocked down by a wave, it just pops back up, and if the hatches are closed, it floats like a bubble on the surface. So I didn't have any fear about the voyage, instead I was worried what the stress would do to our relationship.

The boys took their watches competently and I was handling things well in the galley. We decided to skip Sabine Pass and head directly to New Orleans. Just as we had decided to go for it, the wind decided to go for it, too. It kicked up to 20, then 25 knots. Then we discovered that the sailmaker had missed one of our most important repairs on the main sail, which started coming off the track. It was getting really rough. Everything in the cabin was flying through the air. The bungie cords hadn't held the cabinets.

Then we saw the lightening, which revealed a massive storm system directly in our path. We turned south in hopes of missing it. Then the flashes became constant, with three to four strikes at a time. We hooked the battery charger cables to the mast and hung them overboard to ground us if we were hit. Finally, we had weathered the lightning, but it was so rough that waves were coming into the cockpit. We were on two-hour watches, and Patrick and I were topside when the wind hit 30 knots. Fortunately, we had put up the small storm sail, so we could still have steerage—very important at all times (no steerage, equals being hit broadside). Our safety harnesses were clasped, but it was impossible to function. The waves were 10 to 12 feet high. The cabin was in turmoil. We fought the winds for six hours in the dark. When below, we were tossed like rag dolls across the cabin, with bruised elbows, shins and hips. It was uncomfortable, but we were OK.

Then I noticed faint flashes in the distance, and the fear struck, lightening again from two storms, one to starboard and one to port, in other words, half the horizon. It was 3:30 a.m. Finally, we woke up Terry. We had to yell for him to hear over the noise of the wind. He decided to turn and backtrack, but that tack turned out to be so rough, we couldn't manage it. We were being thrown around like corks in a blender. We were going 9 knots which was actually beyond the hull speed of the boat. Terry had never seen it move this fast. He decided we had to heave to, which ties the tiller over to one side, and the sail tied over to the other side. This puts the brakes on, so we could batten the hatches and go below. It looked like a bomb had gone off in the cabin. There was no place to lie down, so we just climbed on top of the mess and collapsed. It was 5:30 a.m. The bow was bouncing so much that our bodies would leave the bed with each wave. Fortunately, we were too tired to care.

Suddenly we were all thrown out of the berths as the boat received a knock-down, which is when a boat is knocked on its side by wind or waves. Then the boat righted itself and we were up. It was 8:30 a.m. and we had missed the two big storms. The sky was clear and the wind dropped to 25 knots, and we could *see* in daylight.

Adam and I went on watch so Terry could sleep. When he came up, I collapsed. I couldn't hold on anymore. The adrenaline had kept me strong, but now I was totally weak and my knees shook. We had blown off course, so we headed back to Sabine Pass. We had lost a day and a night and were back where we had decided to go to New Orleans. All that work and drama for nothing. We dove into the chocolate chip cookies which worked their "medicinal" magic. "Now I get it." I said.

It was June 30th, Daddy's birthday, and we decided to move into the Intracoastal Waterway so we could make repairs and put everything back together. This is where we saw our first alligators, three big ones swimming in our direction. That was eerie. I was so proud of how well our boys had handled everything! Wow, they were amazing troopers.

Within an hour, the engine started dying because the water

pump was overheating. Terry tore into everything in an attempt to fix it. Finally, he started pouring cold water onto the pump, so we took turns. The extra water could be pumped out from the bilge. We got the boat cleaned up just as we pulled into Orange, Texas at 6:00 p.m. There was an old 1950's motel called the Orange House Inn, painted bright aqua and orange, on the water, with MUSAK "music" blaring out over a rickety dock and a deserted turning-basin filled with rusty barges. The boys went in to register—$8 per night to dock—and came back crestfallen because there were no shower facilities. But they did have a huge old swimming pool. We called out for pizza, took a swim and called Daddy and wished him, "Happy Birthday!" I found a water hose on the dock, and in my bathing suit, washed my hair and took a bath, in front of God and everyone. We were all so tired, we couldn't sleep.

The MUSAK played all night and the mosquitoes returned to the boys, escaping the heat on deck. The next morning, Adam caught a catfish with a piece of salami on his hook, and we opened a can of bacon and scrambled eggs and fried the catfish. Peace! Later that morning, we ran into a kid named, "Sham," who took us to get ice and Waterway Charts in his new black Corvette. He was 16 and had made $40,000 last summer selling TV Dishes to people who couldn't get Cable. Our boys were in awe. Sham gave them a spin. We finally cast off at 11:00 and landed at the Calcasieu Locks in Louisiana at 7:00 p.m., after running aground in the shallow water and getting pulled off by a Cajun shrimper, who called us, "Lil sell boaat." We anchored, had a dinner of cooked cabbage and ham and I gave Terry a haircut. Adam caught another catfish. Right then, I realized Adam would never go hungry, which was a relief. I put up my new screens, so NO mosquitos! This was the first real sleep we had gotten. We were getting the hang of it.

These were just the first few days of our crossing the Gulf of Mexico, which lasted a total of 44 days. Such days were typical of the whole journey, filled with every imaginable happening, and running the gamut of every emotion. Patrick would be leaving on July 15th, and Adam on August 3rd, to return to their schools. The boys had learned life lessons which can only be taught by going to sea. They had seen primordial jungles and swamps, which looked like the beginning of time, with unusual birds, alligators, and big snakes swimming in the water. They had learned naval navigation and how to read charts. And, that a 10' deep channel on the charts, can actually be only 5' deep and the boat can run aground. They had met a Cajun shrimper Captain, who came out of his way to pull us off a sand bar, just as the tide was going out and our boat was leaning precipitously on it's side. The water was just inches from flooding us.

They had learned to fish and dive for scallops for their dinner. Adam also learned how to get a big stingray, with a poisonous stinger, off his hook. They learned to drive the dinghy by themselves, and pull the anchor and steer with the tiller. They also had begun to appreciate simple things: fresh showers, refrigeration, electricity and clean clothes. They had sailed the great Mississippi and Lake Pontchartrain, and listened to the old-timers play real New Orleans jazz in Preservation Hall. They saw only *some* of the wild sights on Bourbon Street, another partial rite of passage. They had felt the exhilaration of seeing the dolphins riding the bow wave of our boat and catching the rare sight of a manatee while snorkeling. They got to experience life without TV... the REAL life that only nature and its incredible sights and sunsets can offer. They had felt the fear of danger and had seen how families must cooperate in harsh circumstances, and that sometimes life rests on a wing and a prayer. They would remember and understand the benefits of these experiences for the rest of their lives. So would I.

In Pensacola, we had to get Patrick to the airport to meet his schedule. Thankfully, we were offered a ride from fellow sailors at the dock and got to see Fort Barancas, built by the Spanish in 1559. Patrick was really sad to leave. He talked of maybe having a "family reunion" at Christmas. He was certainly a more mature and seasoned young man now. He had been an outstanding crew member and we all got tears in our eyes as he and Adam parted like brothers.

The Florida beaches are white crystal with clear green and turquoise waters. Seeing them made me realize that we were actually manifesting our dream. It was really happening! And, I was going to be a fine artist again, come hell or high water.

Finally, on day 36, we arrived in Tarpon Springs, Florida, a Greek fishing and sponging village. We got our first mail, and Adam got a glimpse of the old days, when news took weeks or months to travel. We saw our first flying fish and I discovered that my breast tumor had returned. I was going to have to face more tests soon. Adam got his wish of going deepsea fishing and he caught 30 fish! He was delighted! This gift was my expression of my gratitude for all that he had done, and the Grand Finale of his trip.

On day 38, August 3rd, Adam left to fly home. Unfortunately, we were only a three day sail from Key West, so he was going to miss that. He had been with us for 44 days and had been an amazing trooper. He had also been the clown of the trip and his antics and humor had kept us laughing and our spirits high on some of the darkest days. It was so hard to say goodbye! I felt so proud of the courageous and strong young man that he had become. I was also thrilled at how we had bonded, after our long time apart. Our deep conversations had meant so much to each of us. I think he had gotten a really good idea of who his mom really is, which developed a new respect between us both. He had a new confidence, from a wealth of life experiences under his belt. Thankfully, Adam had gotten much more than a trip. He was on his way. Go with God, my handsome son! I love you, darling Adam!

Landfall in Key West was just the next chapter in my two year saga of sailing on the Rebel with Terry Duff. I loved our many exciting adventures and astounding experiences, which would completely fill another book. But, I began to realize that running away wasn't working. Maybe after the terror of cancer, I had easily

The Pier House Hotel in Key West, where we moored and ran a charter boat business.

been brave enough to cross the Gulf of Mexico in a 36-foot boat. But, the tumor was back. Now, I wanted to live life to the extreme and feel the whole gamut of emotions, just in case life was getting shorter.

At this point, we both needed an income, so I paid $700 to start our sailing charter business. I also created our tour schedule, and wrote and designed our promotional brochures. We took tourists out for champagne sunsets and snorkel trips to a deserted island. I loved teaching snorkeling and witnessing people's first sight of the tropical fish, brilliant living jewels, among the brightly patterned corals. It was a hard life, but a refreshing healthy one.

It was here that Ali got her trip that I had promised. When we picked her up at the airstrip and she saw me, she was surprised that my red hair had sun-bleached to platinum blonde. She thought that I had bleached it on purpose. She could only stay one week so we packed it full of everything Key West had to offer. I was thrilled to see her make lists of the wonderful things she saw. Since she had missed the crossing, I read her my journal at night, so she got a blow-by-blow vicarious voyage. She was fascinated. She loved her first snorkel, seeing the gorgeous tropical fish. I took her to see Mel Fisher's treasure from the sunken Spanish ship, The Atocha, which had tons of gold and silver bricks on display. She enjoyed the Key West Aquarium. I hated to have such a brief visit, but I had gotten used to them. I treasure any time that I get with my darlings. She flew out on a little six-seat airplane and later exclaimed about the beauty of the turquoise waters she had seen from the air. Sadly, she returned to school in Houston. At least she had gotten a taste of the tropics, and I hoped there would be more. I love you, my darling Alethea!

Terry had gotten several good freelance photography jobs and I had several illustration and graphics commissions. Later that season, we were lucky that we hadn't headed directly to the Bahamas. We survived Kate, a huge hurricane, with 110 knot winds, by tying the boat to a floating dock. The storm surge rose over 8 feet when it hit, and the noise in the boat was like being under a freight train for eight hours. Visibility from the ports was nil, nothing but whipping cream in a blender. The boat bounced up and down 7 feet with every wave.

After the storm, we took inventory. We were covered with scrapes and bruises. We were so lucky that we still had a boat/home and our charter business. Many neighbors lost everything!

Our business was good because the Pier House Hotel was our concierge and sent us the nicest clients. However, it was very demanding physically, especially as a fulltime job and we were on the boat 24/7. Plus, I think we both were suffering from extreme fatigue and heat exhaustion. This was putting a huge strain on the relationship. We argued a lot. After teaching snorkeling for months, I developed an inner ear infection, with severe vertigo, so I had to move off the boat for a month. This added an additional strain. Because of my cancer scare, I was focusing on being really healthy, so I decided to stop drinking alcohol on August 14th, 1985. This presented an even bigger challenge to the relationship, because sailors love to drink. "Yo, ho, ho and a bottle of rum!"

Terry announced that he wanted to stay in Key West and give up our Bahamas Dream. I still wanted to travel. The whole world was out there waiting, and time was of the essence for me. Terry was enjoying financial success, so he never wanted to take a day off from the constant pressure. We were seriously drifting apart. The beautiful tropics had become a grind. My dream of being a fine artist was fading fast.

Finally, fate intervened. The lump in my breast had grown really fast. I called my surgeon in Austin and he said to return immediately. I packed all my belongings and drove 28 hours back to Texas. I stopped in Houston for a short while to see my kids. In Austin, I stayed with Mom and Dad, and after the surgery, I got the same diagnosis, fibrocystic sarcoma again. Mom and Dad freaked out.

All I needed was time and peace to think. My dearest friend, Janice, offered a spare bedroom and I thankfully accepted. I was there for a month, trying to get my head on straight. If I were dying, I certainly would not burden my children because they had been through enough already. I checked on possible graphics jobs, but the recession had forced cutbacks and even flight to jobs out of state for my former colleagues. Unfortunately, my source of income was back in Florida and I wasn't up to the physical demands right away. I felt caught. At night, I would be dreaming of being on the water, and when I awoke, I was in a room so far away. I would burst into tears.

Land life seemed so static, the air was "conditioned," and the Earth, concrete and pavement. I realized that I had become addicted to nature, the sea, the sun, and the wind. I was a fish out of water and literally miserable. I could easily understand why the old sailors had reenlisted over and over, in spite of the hardships and meager pay. The sea's salt is actually running in our veins. Maybe it was a primordial memory still in our DNA and the sea draws us emotionally back to our original life-giving origins? All I knew was that the sea had changed me.

I had been in Austin about seven weeks. Terry wanted to meet in Santa Barbara for Christmas and to introduce me to his two brothers. Afterwards, we would travel back to the boat together. I felt serious reservations, but he had invited Patrick, so I agreed. Maybe it would be OK?

Santa Barbara was a disaster. We argued numerous times during the five days! I couldn't believe it. Nothing was ever enough. For once, I refused to let myself be subjected to any more negativity! Period! I stood up for myself.

The four guys decided to go to a bar, so I was left alone in a strange town, in a strange house, and I had no idea where they were going. I knew it would be very late before they returned. I came to my senses. Our combative relationship was never going to work. That was it!

Maybe Terry had forgotten that I had a brother in California? I called Lew and told him my plight. Lew said to go to the airport and he would pick me up in his private plane. He was a film producer in Hollywood and had been a private pilot with his own plane for years. My rental car was on my credit card, and I needed to return it anyway. So, I grabbed my bag, and left.

Lew flew me to his home in Granada Hills, with a beautiful pool and a view of the city. I was so deeply grateful for his caring and generous hospitality, and for even entertaining me! We flew out over the Pacific to see the magnificent grey whales, and to San Diego for lunch and to see the famous tall ship, "The Star of India." His passion was airplanes and mine was boats. He flew me up to Yosemite for three days, where I had the most amazing dreams of a spiritual figure, which I called "The Grand Contemplator." He looked like a monk and I could ask him questions. He was sitting cross-legged in a crystal pyramid and all sorts of amazing visions occurred. In one dream, energy came into me and I was told that I was a healer, and from now on, I was to act only from a loving state. My physical body and my spiritual essence merged and I became "light" itself. I hoped that perhaps these signaled that I had attained a higher level of enlightenment. All I knew was that I felt dazed afterwards.

Lew was so sweet. He even took me to a party for the cast of the TV show, "Laugh-In," and I met all the famous stars. I even met the movie star, Michael Landon in Malibu, during one of Lew's filming jobs. So, things had definitely improved! Lew wanted me to stay in California. I was so grateful to him for rescuing me and his kindnesses, but I just couldn't settle my mind. I didn't contact Terry again. I let him keep our business, even though I had put 1½ years of work and considerable money into it. I realized that our relationship was finished. But, in looking back, I could see all the benefits that I had received and I was truly thankful to Terry for the amazing experiences that I had.

Sailing had made my life exciting and heightened my senses. The challenges had given me a physical confidence, independence, and had grounded me to Earth. I had developed endurance and a fearlessness. I discovered that I liked living "on the edge," always in suspense of what might be coming up next. It made me feel truly *alive*. So, *thank you*, Terry Duff, for the incredible blessings that had truly changed me at depth.

Now back to the real world: I was in California with no job, no home, no car, no nothing. I couldn't believe it, but I was back to ground zero again! The idea of starting completely over in California was overwhelming. Only seven weeks had passed since my surgery, and during that time, I had experienced four major losses: I had left Terry and in doing so, lost my job and my home, not to mention my dream of

Top: My brother, Lew Valentine Adams, film producer; bottom: Lew and wife, Louise, at their wedding.

being an artist.

I was in shock. Actually I was utterly heart broken, and felt so empty inside. Another important romantic relationship had failed. It seemed that no matter what I worked for, nor cared about, it was eventually taken away. It seemed like my life was just one "burglary scene" after another. Yet, I was determined to resist being in the role of a victim. That was repugnant to me. So, instead, I began asking: "Why? What is the Universe trying to tell me or teach me? What is this pattern? What can I do to take responsibility and change? What is my life's purpose? What is my true spiritual quest? Why was I given my artistic gifts, and yet they were thwarted or squandered? What the hell does it all mean? Who am I?" My questions were endless. Of course, they were the great existential questions that everyone must ask at some time in their lives… or not. This was my turning point. All my life, I had set goals and made plans and worked as hard as I could to be a success. I had to let go. I couldn't carry it all anymore. And, at that moment, I became a "seeker." I gave up my Western mind, the logical approach to life. Besides, it hadn't really worked very well for me... had it?

Months earlier, back in Key West, I had gone to counseling. The counselor had seemed "psychic" because she had told me my whole life story, after only a few minutes. She introduced me to the concept of being "codependent," one who aligns with compulsive partners, and then tries to rescue them. It is common in many addictive relationships, involving alcoholics, drug users, and others who have compulsive disorders. Evidently, I was a codependent, so I begun studying everything I could find on the subject. Actually, it was fascinating and explained so many of my behaviors and issues. This was my 'mind-set' when I had left Key West for my surgery. As I continued studying, I was discovering some important answers to my big existential questions. I was taking responsibility, and in the process, I was finding *myself*. My explorations turned inward. Instead of examining Life, I was examining ME. It struck me that maybe that's what Socrates had meant when he said, "The unexamined life was not worth life living." Maybe it was examining outside *and inside*? Maybe the Universe was emptying me, so that I could find the *real* me, my spiritual self?

All I knew was that I had to follow my own inner guidance now. I turned my life over to my instincts, my hunches, my gut, which I now realized was "following my heart." I couldn't make any plans. I would just wait until the right opportunity or direction presented itself. I truly did not know what else to do. I surrendered and gave my fate to the Universe. I called my dearest friend, Nonie, in hopes of visiting her in La Jolla, while I was still in California. As friends do, I told her my whole tale of woe. She was great, giving me needed emotional support. She had lived in Maui, Hawaii for 15 months and said that it was a wonderful experience.

Then she said, "Zilla! You should go to Maui! Really, it's exactly what you need…Go to Maui!" The words literally hit me! Chills began running up and down my body. The hair on my arms stood out. What on Earth was happening? I told her, and she repeated, "Just go to Maui!"

The next day, I asked Lew to take me to the airport. He assumed I was headed back to Texas. When he heard me tell the ticket agent, "I want a one way ticket to Maui, Hawaii," his jaw dropped! I thanked him profusely and hugged him. I love you, Lew! At this point, I needed a break. What harm could a little tropical vacation do?

I never looked up Maui on a map. I was following my inner self, that "guidance" that had given my body chills from the inside, out. I had to trust it because no other message, nor direction, nor path had appeared. It was all I had left. Besides, if I were actually dying, at least my children would not witness it, and I would have a beautiful tropical place to depart in peace. This was not being dramatic, because back in the 80's, a second reappearance of cancer was a death sentence, especially one growing so rapidly.

As I settled into the seat on the plane, I thought about Nonie talking about Haleakala Volcano, which was on Maui. She had called it: "The heart chakra of the Mother Earth." I had learned about the "chakras," the energy centers in the human body, known in ancient Asia, China and India. The idea of the Earth having a heart chakra was compelling to me. Maybe it could heal my own heart? Maybe that's why I was going to Maui?

In California, I had gone with my artist friend, Mary Pillot, to the Bode Tree book store, a "new-age," metaphysical book shop made famous by the actress, Shirley MacLaine. A book, *Ano, Ano, the Seed*, by Kristin Zambucka, had caught my eye. Kristin had been knighted by the Queen of England for this book and it had beautiful paintings of ancient Hawaiians on the cover, so I bought it. I carried it with me, in my one suitcase filled with boat clothes. In those days, there were no direct flights to Maui, so I stayed with my dear friend, Cherry Walts, in Oahu for a few days. It was lovely, but I was still wanting Maui. Cherry took me to the airport. Thank you, dear friend, for your sweet hospitality! Hello, Maui!

My plane landed at night, so I couldn't see much. When I asked the rental car lady, she said, "You are in Kahului," and I started laughing! "Ka- hu"- What?" The whole thing suddenly seemed unbelievably funny to me. Why was I laughing? Was I finally following my bliss? She gave me a little map which I put in my purse. I was just going to follow my instincts and see where I landed. As I arrived at an intersection, I asked, "Right or Left?" and then turned where my hunch indicated. As crazy as this sounds, it was almost a game to me. Very soon, I could smell the ocean! Oh my God, my beautiful Pacific! My "guidance" had led me straight to the harbor. I got tears in my eyes as I ripped off my shoes and waded into the shallow water. I wept as I stood still, letting its energy flow into me. Tears of joy streamed down my face. I was saved! I felt total peace listening to the waves and feeling the gentle breeze caress my face, as if it were saying, "It's all going to be all right." I was reconnected at last to my beloved Natural world, the real world. "Thank you, Divine Mother Earth, my real mother."

I found a little 1950's style motel a short distance away and checked in. I took a shower and washed my hair. As I was brushing, it suddenly hit me…What had I done? I was 2,000 miles from anyone I knew, in the middle of the Pacific Ocean, with very little money, no friends, no job, no car, no home, no address, not even a phone number. And I didn't even know where I was on a map. I must be crazy! I started to cry. I cried for about two minutes and then I yelled, "NO! STOP IT!" I refuse to be sad. I am strong and I will figure it out! I got into bed and pulled the sheet up to my chin. I lay there very resolute and smiling.

BRIIING!!! BRIING!! The phone rang and I nearly jumped out of my skin! It must be the desk clerk. A man's voice asked, "Is this Zilla?" "Yes, this is Zilla," I said. The man said, "Well, you don't know me, my name is Brad Weber and I'm a friend of Nonie's and she said you might be coming to Maui, and I'm a jeweler in Lahaina, and I get off work at 9:00, and it will take me about 45 minutes to get there, and I drive a BMW, so would you like to go out for a pizza and a beer as a welcome? There is also a birthday party in Haiku tonight, so would you like to go?"

My mouth was hanging open! Not a living soul on this Earth knew where I was. I didn't even know where I was! This was impossible! Utterly impossible! I was speechless! Brad said, "Zilla?" and I said, "Ah, yes. . . yes, that would be great. I'll be ready at 9:45." He said, "Great, I'll see you then."

I was still stunned, but I jumped up and put on makeup and my best shorts outfit. I pondered what had happened? Finally, I decided *not* to ask for an explanation, because I was afraid it might break the "magic spell."

Brad was really good looking, and gentlemanly. We chatted over the pizza and drove into the jungle to the birthday party for a girl who was leaving the island, which was weird, because I was arriving. A sort of switch in positions. We arrived, and the house was in a tree! Yes, the house was the most amazing I'd ever seen, a real adult tree house, on several levels, and covered with giant ivy, and filled with orchids. I ate birthday cake, thinking that I was having a "birthday," a "re-birth day" of sorts, and I listened to ukulele music and singing in Hawaiian, and I laughed my heart out. My Maui life had begun! This is an actual, *true story* of my arrival in Maui, and I never did find out how Brad knew where to find me. . . I just let the magic be. I was to discover that the Islands are much more than magical, and that my life was about to change in profound and remarkable ways. *E komo mai*, Zilla! Welcome!

On my second day in Maui, I found Haleakala Volcano on my map. I packed warm clothes and drove to the top, 10,024 feet above

Above: Beautiful Maui waterfall in the jungle. At right: The crater rim of Haleakala ("The House of the Sun"), the dormant volcano on Maui.

sea level. It was freezing, with 28-knot winds blowing an icy fog and drizzle. The road had been a harrowing experience, with double hairpin turns and no guard rails. The parking lot was utterly deserted, with no sign of life at the Ranger Station. The wind increased and I walked and climbed over large rocks towards the crater rim. The fog blocked sight into the crater, but I didn't care, because I was on a spiritual journey. I wanted to sense the "heart chakra" of Mother Earth and heal my own heart. I found a place between two large boulders and sat with the intension of meditating until I got a "message" or a "sign." The howling wind and blowing fog blotted out any interferences, and I quickly went into an astral state, deep into my inner spiritual being-ness. There was no concept of time. I began to feel an intense energy filling my body with heat. The heat continued to build. I took off my mittens, then my knit hat and my jacket. Finally, I took off my blouse, baring my heart to the Mother Earth. My body started rocking and slowly pulsating in a circular motion. I felt no cold whatsoever. My body started to turn into energy and my molecules blended into the air molecules and the molecules of the rocks and rain. I became one with everything on an energetic level, my atoms swirling with all the other atoms, in absolute *oneness with all existence*. Oneness in consciousness and mind, oneness in awareness. The air had a consciousness. The water had a consciousness. The rocks had a consciousness. The Mother Earth was revealing her heart to me. I was not a separate being. I was Life itself. All time stood still...it was eternal. Nothing mattered, but this knowingness. I was connected and yet I was free. Truly free at last! I was finally at home on this planet. I was blessed. I could begin again, fresh and alive, unburdened from the past. I was strong again and armed with the lessons from the wind and water and earth....a sailor, making landfall on a mountain top. My anchor had dropped. I was home at last!

I thanked the Divine Universal Consciousness in a tearful

prayer, and pulled myself together. I was dazed but felt a new strength. As I descended Haleakala, the House of the Sun, I wept away all my grief, an amazing release.

Swaying palm trees, plumeria and hot pink bougainville greeted me as I reached sea level and my little hotel. The sunset was spectacular and I slept like a baby in my new island paradise. It was many months before I learned that the Hawaiians believe that everything in Life has a consciousness, even inanimate things are conscious. I could certainly agree, for I had gotten the same exact knowingness from the Earth Mother, herself! I had been introduced to the Ancient Hawaiian's reality and their love of their beloved "AINA," the Mother Earth, the most profound experience! I had followed my instincts and my heart to Haleakala, and it had proven to be the correct move. I was beginning to know myself and to trust my inner guidance. This, and Maui, were to lead me to extraordinary developments and growth for the next 25 years. Aloha, nui loa, Maui! I love you very much!

On the third day, I decided to call the only phone number that Nonie had given me, a lady named Darlene De Mello. I introduced myself, saying, "You don't know me, but I'm Zilla Adams, a friend of Nonie's and she gave me your number." Darlene replied, "You're a friend of Nonie's, great! Come on over to Lahaina, there is a birthday party at the Yacht Club, so just park and come on in! Any friend of Nonie's is a friend of mine!"

Wow! These people are very friendly and they must really love Nonie! I got directions and headed west about 17 miles. I didn't realize that Lahaina was a small village and I drove right past the Club. As I turned the car around, I saw the most amazing sight. It

Clockwise from top left: Giant Buddha at the Jodo Mission in Lahaina; Friends: Darlene Demello, Nonie Otto, and I on the beach near Darlene's cottage; Lynn Shue, Stewart Marshall, and Kate, who was leaving her posiition at the Village Gallery in Lahaina, where this picture was taken.

was a huge Buddha statue, peeking over a tall wall. The gate sign said, "Jodo Mission," so I immediately got out of the car and entered the large enclosed garden. There was a tall Pagoda and a Buddhist Church, flowering trees, and a huge gong under a roof.

As I turned, I was face to face with "the Grand Contemplator," the spiritual being in my recent dreams, except he was a giant bronze sculpture on a large concrete platform. I was so surprised that I had a hard time looking directly into his face.

That was so weird. I felt shocked, or nonplussed or something? I said a prayer of gratitude and hurried back to find the Club. Darlene welcomed me as a long lost friend and introduced me to everyone, about ten ladies in the party. Everyone there was so friendly! The Club was built out over the water and nautical flags were flying everywhere. What a festive place! Then I realized I was at *another* birthday party! Another "re-birth" party for me! I immediately got the symbolism! It seemed too coincidental. I guess I was actually going through a re-birthing experience into a new chapter in my life. When I told Darlene where I was staying, she said, "No, No, you can't stay there! I have a little house on the beach in Lahaina and you can stay there until you find your way."

She was so insistent, that I agreed, so after the party, I packed and went to meet Darlene after work. When we arrived at her cottage, I walked into the kitchen and gasped. I was looking out the window directly at the big Buddha! I started laughing. I told Darlene my crazy story and we agreed that all of this was way beyond coincidence! She said it seemed that I was already in the Maui "flow," which I guess meant that Maui had accepted me. She said that sometimes Maui spits people out! Yikes! I suppose we will see?

Darlene's cottage was situated directly between the Jodo Mission and the beach, called Baby (Keiki) Beach because that's where babies learn to swim. She gave me the bedroom facing the ocean, which was about 60 feet away. The beach came right up to her lawn. There was a big covered patio with lounge chairs and tables, and a hammock tied to palm trees, with an outdoor shower. I couldn't believe that I could just walk out the door and swim at the beach! Amazing! Plus, Darlene was the sweetest person in the world. I couldn't have wished for a more perfect, happy roommate!

The only thing she cautioned about was, "Never put your blanket under a coconut palm tree, if one falls, it can kill you!" So far, that was the only negative or dangerous thing in Lahaina. Later, I found out that Lahaina is a World Heritage historic site.

On day four, Darlene went to work at the Yacht Club, so I decided to explore. I walked through the Jodo Mission, said, "Hello" to the Buddha, and decided to follow my nose again. At Front Street, I asked, "Left or Right?" and so, I turned left. I walked two blocks and saw the Village Art Gallery on the water side. I went in and was very impressed with the interesting mix of eclectic, very high-caliber paintings. I mentioned this to Marina Beebe, the art consultant. She was also a fine artist and lived on a boat! She pointed out the window to her boat, which was moored a few hundred yards away. I laughed and said, "How convenient!"

To my amazement, we discovered that we were sorority sisters! She was Alpha Gam at Berkley and I was Alpha Gam at U. Texas! Small world! She then said, "I'm going to tell Lynn to hire you. We need someone, now that Kate is leaving and you would be perfect." What??? She called Lynn at the main Gallery on Dickenson Street and sent me to interview. I rushed home and changed clothes and walked the eight blocks. The Village Gallery on Dickenson was quite large and filled with the works of all the major artists in Hawaii. I was impressed again! It was the oldest gallery in Hawaii. Lynn Shue and I hit it off, and I was hired immediately! Another Maui miracle!

Suddenly I was thrust back into the fine art world and I could really begin painting again! Plus, I would have a venue in which to sell my work! I could hardly believe it. Maui was literally pouring blessings into my arms! I was so filled with gratitude, I said little prayers all the way to the Yacht Club to tell Darlene. She was thrilled that I had gotten a job in such a short time. We laughed and celebrated. She said, "You are definitely a Maui "keeper."

I walked back to the house. The weather was perfect for snorkeling. In fact, the weather always seemed perfect. I looked out to sea and my only hope now was to start sailing again. Right then, there was a knock on the door. It was Judy, a friend of Darlene's, who was the manager of all the boat charters in the Harbor. She said she was delivering a large amount of cash, $20,000 to pay the boat captains and she didn't want to go alone. So, could I accompany her? "Of course," I agreed. As she talked to the captains, she mentioned

Clockwise from far left: I love to paint the features of the Hawaiian people; At my job selling tours at the harbor in Lahaina, I was able to restablish my sea captain's license which I had earned in Florida; My first oil painting done in Maui is my love letter to the Pacific Ocean.

that I also had a captain's license. They replied, "A six Pack?" (six passengers).

I replied, "No, a 50-ton Ocean Operator's License." Well, that really turned some heads. I felt very proud. (Back at the Captain's Exam in Miami, there had been 300 men there, and I was the only woman, so that was quite an achievement, "for a girl"). We continued delivering funds around the Harbor.

At a kiosk called Pier One we met a woman named Louise Rocket, who owned the charter. We both laughed when we discovered that she had also lived on a boat and chartered in Key West! Another small world! I told her I would need sea-time in order to switch my license from Florida to Maui County. She offered me a job booking tours, on the spot! I could sell tours for numerous Charter boats, which would give me access to *all* the boats. In fact, that was a job requirement, so I could understand what I was selling. Unbelievable! I had to laugh, because I couldn't wait to tell Darlene that I had gotten TWO perfect jobs in one day! Even she would be amazed. I had never seen anything like this. Life was supposed to be hard work and a struggle. I had never been welcomed like this in my life! My new home was truly a paradise in every way. I also wanted to explore more of Maui because I had never seen such remarkable beauty and variations in the landscape, compressed into

such a small area.

Now that I had two jobs, and I wanted to explore, I needed transportation. My jobs started on February 7th and 11th, so I planned to go to the bike shop, but on the 6th, a friend of Darlene's drove up with a bike in her car! It needed some work, but it only cost $50, so it was perfect. I could easily ride to the Gallery and the Harbor, and also start a little exploring. This bike fulfilled the last of my needs, establishing me as an official, employed resident of Maui, Hawaii! Following my heart was really working! I called Kelly with all my good news, and she promised to mail some boxes of art supplies from my storage. In exchange, I said I would raise some money to bring her to Maui. She was graduating from U Texas in August.

Then I called Ali to tell her all my good news. Unfortunately, she had missed my last call, and I felt bad, so I explained that the time difference is five hours, and Texas is five hours *earlier*, so we wouldn't miss calls again. I also tried to get Adam's contact information, but couldn't? I will try again.

On my first day of work, I sold $1,300 in tours, so hopefully, I was going to be OK financially, too. Hooray! I loved working at the Gallery. too. There were about 90 artists represented and I enjoyed getting to know them. It was so inspiring to be back in a fine arts environment, which was very active and professional. I was amazed to hear that Maui was number four in art sales in the USA.

I set up my easel outside, under Darlene's covered patio, with perfect light and ventilation. My first Maui oil painting was of the tropical ocean, looking down into the water from above. It was abstract, with all the rich blues, aquas, and turquoises that I loved. It was also my "love letter" to the glorious Maui Pacific, and was my "declaration" that *I was a fine artist* again. At last!

I also began plein air painting with several local artists: George Allan, Lowell Mapes, Betty Hay Freeland, Nancy Young, and Marina Beebe. Every Thursday at 4:00 p.m., we would all converge at a chosen location to paint landscapes or seascapes. I couldn't believe how beautiful Maui was! Everywhere I looked, there was a stunning view to be captured. I painted the sea, islands, docks, mountains, jungles, waterfalls, and the most spectacular sunsets, imaginable. It was intoxicating to me! Now, I felt that I truly understood Gauguin's inspiration and his passion as he painted in Tahiti. Me, too!

Every Tuesday after work, we would all meet at George Allan's large studio to draw the nude. We all pitched in to share the model's fees and the potluck meals. Sometimes during our breaks, George would sit down at his grand piano and give us a mini-concert. He was an accomplished pianist, too. Happily, I discovered that I had not lost any of my drawing skills, even if it seemed like a century had passed since I had done life drawing. This was heaven to me. We would all discuss art and share ideas and techniques, which is so important, because being an artist can be a very lonely pursuit. I thought back to the great Movements in art, and how groups of artists knew each other and exchanged ideas and theories, and shared support. So this group became very meaningful to me and my development. I was in awe at how wonderful my life had become!

I was also growing spiritually, which had always been a huge part of my life's quest. I had already begun meditating with crystals and having unusually vivid, prophetic visions. Back in Austin, I had learned some chakra energy healing techniques from Karen Wakeman and Allan Mesher, an attempt to prevent my cancer from returning. I sent energy into my body using my imagination.

Also, in California I had practiced on my brother, Lew, and other friends. As my hands became very hot, they had reported feeling heat and tingling in their hands and feet, and that their pains had disappeared! This was encouraging to me, even if a bit bizarre, because the only "healers" I knew were the ones on TV. I didn't really believe they were genuine. Even so, I felt "called" to learn more, always being an "explorer."

I had heard of the famous Kahuna healers, so I was determined to investigate. I found several books on the subject: *The Heart of the Huna*, by Laura Kealoha Yardly and *Urban Shaman* by Serge Kahili King, Phd. These peeked my curiosity about healing even more. I was hoping to meet a real Kahuna and to learn their treasured secrets. I knew the Hawaiians lived by the practice called "Aloha",

 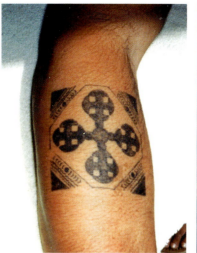 

From left: Bill Aki taught me all about ancient Hawaiian spirituality; Bill's tattoo is a Kahuna symbol; The schooner Machias, a research vessel that sailed the Pacific, was the largest vessel I had ever sailed, and was captained by my friend, Bill Austin. I crewed on this boat for close to three years.

which was to love others like family. I was beginning to believe that their love of the land was also part of the Aloha spirit. I wondered if that explained why the people here, from many different ethnicities and nationalities, got along so well? Is that also why Maui was so beautiful and full of rainbows? It seemed as if the Gods were constantly blessing the land. Did the Kahunas have some special powers to make humankind and nature work together? It certainly seemed that there was something very magical going on here.

One day, as I was leaving the harbor, I saw a large Hawaiian man unloading his guitars from the Windjammer cruise boat. I was immediately intrigued and began talking to him. After our introduction, I saw an unusual tattoo on his arm and I found myself saying, "Bill, you are a Kahuna, aren't you?" He stopped and stared at me, his eyes full of suspicion Then, I said, "I really want to talk to you, so can we get together over lunch or something?"

He held up his guitar between us, as if for protection, and said, "Maybe." Finally, after my extended explanation, he agreed to meet me for breakfast at Moose's. When I arrived the next morning, he had brought three Hawaiian women with him! I smiled at this because it indicated to me that he must, indeed, be a Kahuna. It was well known that Kahunas kept their precious secrets from the "haoles," the white people who were the "takers." With my blond hair and fair skin, I was about as haole-looking as a person could be. After a very long breakfast, he finally agreed to meet with me again, and thus began my three-year apprenticeship with the most spiritual, deepest, kindest, and most devoted Kahuna friend imaginable. We delved into the healing arts, the philosophies, and the ancient Hawaiian beliefs and spirituality.

From all this, I knew in my heart, that I was destined to be a healer. It was equally as important as my path as an artist. Plus, it might just keep me well, so I had an even greater motive to pursue it. Eventually, it was to enrich my life, as much as my art had, which I would never have expected.

I was overwhelmed with a huge feeling of peace and joy in

my heart. The beauty and energy of Maui was feeding my soul. I was finally back to my original "self," the true artist and seeker of knowledge, the "self" before I was married, and had serious responsibilities to others. This "self" was being totally true to me. I felt a delirious sense of freedom, as if my soul had been set free. My heart was singing. I had journeyed for years seeking happiness and trying to find my way—and I had come full circle to find *me*, and happiness at last.

Maybe this was the necessary step I had to take, before my children could be restored to me? I didn't know, but in looking back, it seemed so. About eight months passed and I was on a roll. I worked hard at both jobs, and I learned the gallery business, which for an artist, is essential. I went out on the boats and accrued my seatime to transfer my captain's license.

I was accepted to crew on the famous research ship, the schooner, "Machias," captained by Bill Austin, the sailing legend of the Pacific. He had sailed the whole Pacific and had even discovered underwater volcanoes. This was the largest sailing vessel, 100 feet long, that I had ever sailed. We took tours across the channel to Molokai, which was very exciting because 12 foot waves were pretty standard. I was also able to explore the island and hike to a "Heiau," a huge stone center where the ancient Hawaiians worshipped. When I arrived there, it was a brilliant sunny day, and yet a light rain fell on me, even though there were no clouds! I said a silent prayer for my children and asked to see them again. My Hawaiian friend said that I had gotten a blessing from the Gods, which seemed true. Another blessing was on its way.

One day, back at Darlene's, the phone rang. It was Adam! I hadn't heard from him in months. He said that he had lots to tell me and asked if he could please come to see me in Maui. I said, "Of course, here is my credit card number." Then I added, "Please do one more thing, tell me if you feel any special energy when you get off the plane." He agreed. When I went to the airport to pick him up, his first words were, "I feel it." I said, "What?" He said, "Mom! I feel this incredible energy, I do!" I knew right then that he was also coming home!

Darlene was so kind to let Adam sleep on the sofa until we could find a place to live. Actually, Adam often slept outside in the hammock, a habit he had acquired on the sail boat. I started looking and spreading the word for an available house. A Hawaiian man said there was one on the beach, next to the Omori Compound. I knew I couldn't afford that, but then the answer came. Kelly called, and she had graduated and wanted to come to Maui. That was it! If we all shared the rent, we could swing it. But, neither child had a job yet, so I just had to trust that it would all work out.

I leased the beach house, which was located only four houses from Darlene's. Perfect! I prayed that my trust and my hunch would be correct. To have my kids with me, at last, would be the greatest answer to all my prayers. Maybe, even Ali could come eventually, if I could just make it work.

Kelly arrived, and she, too, could feel the energy. We moved into our new beach house. Kelly and Adam were awestruck at the beauty of Maui and their new home. Her "vacation" eventually stretched into a year. We bonded and grew, and healed together. We all went to counseling of one type or another, which helped us to understand the divorce and other hardships, and to reach closure, both emotionally and spiritually. Kelly got a job in a cute boutique and Adam started work at the Westin Hotel. With my two jobs, and theirs, we combined forces to pay our expenses, and have some fun, too.

We started exploring Maui in Kelly's old clunker car, which she bought soon after her arrival. We had every kind of adventure and fun that Maui offered. We took a helicopter ride over the mountains with waterfalls 1,700 feet high, we soared over Haleakala, and crossed the Channel to Molokai, seeing two huge black Manta Rays, 20' wide, swimming below us. We drove to the luscious jungles of Hana and swam on the black, red, and green beaches. We snorkeled at Molokini Crater, and fed the huge schools of tropical fish. Adam learned to surf right in front of our house. Kelly and I became "beach bunnies," jumping waves and lounging on the sand at the Kaanapali Resorts. Ali eventually came for an extended visit, too, and she got to have some of the same experiences and family bonding, which I had prayed and hoped for her. This was the life

My children, Adam and Kelly (at left), and Alethea on their first days in Maui. Our house on the beach (above), where we all lived together. Kelly is waving from the window.

Ali and I on the beach in Maui, just before we moved to Honolulu.

I had always wanted for my children and it was coming true. My most profound prayers had been answered.

Thank you, Divine Creator, Divine Consciousness, for all these amazing gifts and blessings! Maui had restored me and my family, which was the most precious of my life's desires. We were all now free to live life with positivity and enthusiasm. Life could be exciting and fun, and full of adventure, if we followed our hearts! Malama pono! All was in righteousness!

Kelly had gotten her degree in History, but she wasn't satisfied because her most heartfelt wish was to become a teacher. I encouraged her to follow her heart, so she decided to go back to Texas and get her teaching certificate. It was there that she met her sweetheart, Bob Zabcik. She brought him to Maui to meet me, and he, too, experienced the amazing Hawaiian beauty. I flew to Texas for their wedding, and was able to see darling Ali again, who was back in school in Houston. Adam lived in our beach house with me, off and on, for five years. He studied at Maui Community College and transferred into The University of Hawaii in Honolulu. He got his Bachelors degree there and learned to speak Mandarin Chinese. He travelled extensively to Hong Kong, Thailand, Malaysia, Indochina and Europe. Several years later, back in Maui, he met and married Jessica Jordan, a beautiful girl from Alvin, Texas.

After graduating high school, Ali came to Maui, but she wanted to live in Honolulu, so I landed a job at a large Gallery there. We packed up, moved, and got settled there, but unfortunately, the Gulf War recession had hit and the gallery business was the first to be impacted. Tourism completely halted because the USA was at war and people were afraid to travel. As one gallery closed, I moved to another, and the domino effect began hitting the whole city. Ali decided to return to school in Houston. I couldn't believe this was happening again. External circumstances had wrecked our chance of being together. I was very devastated, but at least we had three months together and she had worked and matured. She had learned a lot about life and what she wanted. She would be going back to college soon, so it was all okay. Ali eventually went to nursing school and became a trauma nurse, working in prestigious Houston hospitals. I am so proud that she also chose to become a healer!

With all my children safely on their paths, and their futures looking promising and bright, I felt a gratifying sense of accomplishment. It wasn't perfect, but neither is life. And, of course, neither am I. We all try to do our best in the circumstances we are dealt. At least, they had gotten education, travel, cultural experiences, lessons in life and the benefits of exposure to the beautiful Hawaiian Aloha Spirit. Love concours all!

I moved back to my beloved Maui, and back to my job at Village Gallery. I was to continue living in Maui for another 19 years, with discoveries and adventures that would easily fill another book. My development as an artist continued, as well as my expertise and recognition as a healer. In 1995, I began my training and was certified as a Healing Touch Practitioner in 1998, working in all the major hospitals in Hawaii. I helped to create the Kaiser Permanente Clinics' First Healing Touch Clinic, and was the director there for three years in Maui. (In 2012, after moving to Palo Alto, California, I practiced Healing Touch in Stanford Medical Center's Healing Partners Program, working on their cancer patients for six months. I also earned my masters degree in clinical/medical hypnotherapy there.)

In 2010, I stayed true to my art career, ending up as the manager of Village Gift and Fine Art, the Village Gallery's Front Street location. My art works were shown in Maui Museums and numerous exhibitions. My paintings have sold for many years and have travelled to homes and offices all over the world.

I also traveled extensively, and for the Millennium 2000, I went to Kathmandu, Nepal to see Mount Everest. I was brought to tears during this monumental experience. Nepal was utterly inspirational. I even visited a Tibetan refugee camp, temples full of monkeys and the ancient city of Baktupur. I brought home a collection of beautiful Tibetan Mandalas painted in 24k gold. I also went to Japan, Taiwan, and Thailand. The Sultan's Palace in Bangkok was like being in the glittering City of Oz. For the Kathmandu trip, I am eternally grateful to my dear friend, Tim Liphold, for his expertise as an amazing guide. He made the trip extraordinary. In 2006, I was invited to Glastonbury, England, to the Goddess Conference with 400 healers from all over the world, and I was written up in the Bristol newspaper.

In Scotland, I traced my children's Witherspoon genealogy and even found the plaque to John Witherspoon, the signer of the American Declaration of Independence, in his home town, Haddington. To find it, I had to hire a car and follow the 17th Century maps given to me at the Scottish Genealogy Office in Edinburgh.

In 2009, I returned to Paris to spend ten days in the museums. Then on to the south of France, where I studied Prehistoric Art History in the Masters Class, from Wisdom University, San Francisco, with my dear friend and professor, Apela Colorado, Phd. We went into Lascaux II Cave and 13 other prehistoric caves,

In 2000, I traveled to Katmandu, Nepal, to see Mt. Everest. In the ancient city of Baktupur in the Himalayas, I visited this Buddhist temple.

to study the art of our ancestors: 35,000 year old paintings and artifacts left by the cave people. That was truly an astounding artistic and spiritual experience. The energy inside the caves was so strong, I thought I might leave my body!

An aerial view of Maui, showing the incredible beauty of the island.

Then I went to Spain, to Barcelona to study Gaudi, Dali and spend two days in the fabulous Picasso Museum. Then to Madrid to visit the Prado Museum for three days, eight hours per day. What an astonishing collection. The Spanish artists have often been the leaders in the history of modern art.

On another trip to Australia, with my dear friend, Jennifer Keller, I had two quests in mind: First, to study Aboriginal art; and second, to try to meet Aboriginal healers. She and I covered half the country, and in Sydney, I met with a group of indigenous healers. We snorkeled the Great Barrier Reef, and in the desert at Uluru (Ayers Rock), I felt the most amazing electromagnetic energy of my life. I returned home from Alice Springs with an incredible collection of 23 captivating Aboriginal paintings. Traveling is one of my favorite adventures because I can combine my love of art and healing together for a richer experience.

At present, I have been to 26 countries, including: Mexico, Canada, The Netherlands, Italy, Austria, Luxembourg, Switzerland, Germany, France, Belgium, England, The Greek Islands, Crete, Puerto Rico, Yugoslavia, Macedonia, Slovenia, Serbia, Croatia, Liechtenstein, The Hawaiian Islands (which were historically another kingdom), Japan, Taiwan, Thailand, Kathmandu, Nepal, Scotland, and Spain. All of these adventures have been lovingly recorded in my 111 personal journals and photographs. I intend to continue many more exciting journeys.

Looking back, I have learned numerous valuable lessons. First, that my children and grand children have been my greatest treasure and joy. They've been the inspiration for me to write my story, in hopes of passing on a little wisdom and leaving them with more than just a memory.

My daughter, Kelly Valentine Witherspoon, and her husband, Robert Zabcik, gave me my grandchildren: Ryan Robert, and Katheryn Ann. Son, Adam Joseph Witherspoon, and his wife, Jessica Jordan, gave me a grandson, Avery Jordan Witherspoon. Daughter, Alethea (Ali) Katherine Witherspoon, gave me granddaughters, Mackenzie Mary Riedle, and Savannah Valentine Witherspoon Anthony, and my grandson, William Witherspoon Anthony. They are the lights of my life.

I have also written this book to possibly give hope to young girls who dream of becoming successful fine artists, and who find very few female mentors in this male-dominated art world. I know how daunting it felt for me, to have so few famous women artists to emulate. It wasn't until I was 34 years old in 1976, when the authors and art historians, Karen Peterson and J. J. Wilson, gave a lecture on women artists at the University of Texas. There I discovered the *true histroy* of female artists. They had just published a book, *Women Artists, Recognition and Reappraisal from the Early Middle Ages to the Twentieth Century,* and I learned there were literally hundreds of women artists who had been *left out* of the art history books. These two women had spent years researching and going into storage attics and basements of the world's museums, and had discovered thousands of amazing works hidden away from public view. With no mention in the art history books, and their works stashed away, *it was as if these gifted women artists had never existed*! And, as if they had been forgotten on purpose!

I was furious, of course. I vowed to do whatever I could to rectify this tragic injustice to the women of the world. So, this was also my reason to write, in hopes that my contemporary story might inspire my own family members, or any young girl or boy, to be fearless and strike out on their most rewarding art journey. To those who do, I say: Never, never give up. The beauty and excitement of art will bring you great joy, enrich your life, and feed your soul.

Don't let fear hold you back from your goals in your life or your art. Renounce fear and simply decide to have faith that the Universe will support you. After all, you are here on earth for some reason, so it's easy to believe in the validity of life itself and be optimistic.

You can choose to live in fear or in faith. You can choose to be positive or negative. If you choose to think positively, you will create positive outcomes. Remember that one of the most amazing gifts we have is free will, the right to choose. And also the power to change our minds—to "un-choose." We choose to be victims or victors. We choose our attitudes and our growth. One of my favorite quotes is, "Life is change, growth is optional... choose wisely."

One of my wisest choices was to learn to meditate. It offers tools to open doors of perception and guidance. If you ask questions of the Universe, you will receive answers, which come as hunches, intincts, or as a small voice from inside yourself. Trusting in that guidance is absolutely vital because it's coming from your own inner wisdom, your heart and soul.

Meditation in closely related to prayer, which I have done all my life. Prayer sends out requests to the Universe for answers, sometimes miraculous ones. I have witnessed this power again and again.

Prayer has taught me that tragedies and troubles are often great lessons which teach us endurance, patience, strength, confidence, and how to overcome and triumph. They grow our charater, align our ethics, and often reveal our paths in life. Recovering from cancer, I realized that the experience had initiated my quest to become a healer and ultimately to work in energy medicine. It also developed a deep compassion in me for those who are suffering—another important facet of spiritual growth.

When you find your life's work, you will have learned to be true to yourself. For me, this helped me find my inner spirit and gave me deep peace and strength. I want to leave the world a better place... and to remain an adventurer.... and to stay curious! Don't wait until retirement to go to Paris or Australia or Kathmandu. You won't enjoy Europe on crutches! Travel has a massive impact on your personal development and ability to be a "citizen of the world."

For me, examining the *outer* world and the *inner* world is the path that brings great harmony, happiness, and peace. That is the whole point of being alive.

Socrates was correct! ***The examined life is truly worth living!*** So... *Go*! Examine, explore, adventure, investigate, question, learn, write, travel, love. Keep an open mind and and be fearless! Trust your curiosity and your guidance. They will lead you to live life and love life, and be the miracle that you are!

ALOHA KAKOU!* "*I LOVE YOU ALL!

The Works

CHAPTER ONE

Life drawings

Throughout the ages, artists have studied the human figure as a primary approach to learning to draw from life. The figure tells the human story, thus it has been the most fundamental subject for the beginning artist. Of course, in recent times, the camera has changed some approaches, but to really learn to draw life, one must draw real living things.

Figure drawing requires many skills, plus intense and accurate observation. One must draw what is actually seen, not what one believes is there. It requires the basic knowledge of anatomy, proportions, movement, negative space and composition. There are also very subtle things to observe and master, such as the delicate shading of the skin, hair, and contours, and capturing the expressions and gestures. To me, this is demanding, compelling, and absolutely fascinating!

I began by copying the anatomy studies of the early anatomists, Vesalius (1553) and Albinus (1770). I also copied drawings by the old Masters, including Michelangelo, Leonardo da Vinci, Raphael, and Rubens. I even studied medical text books. My favorite book is Stephen Rogers Peck's "Atlas of Human Anatomy for the Artist" by Oxford Press.

By age 18, I had already been drawing the figure for six years, and during my freshman year, my drawings were exhibited in the halls of the University of Texas Art Building. My passion and my practice had paid off. For the rest of my life, I have used all of these same skills for any artistic endeavor, whether for architectural renderings, commercial illustration or graphic design.

It's also important to work in all materials: pencil, ink, charcoal, pastel, and paint to convey the many nuances and moods of the human form.

> *"The figure tells the human story."*
> —Zilla Adams
>
> *"The human body is the best work of art."*
> —Jess C. Scott

Two classic life drawings: studies in ballpoint pen, drawn when I was 12 years old.

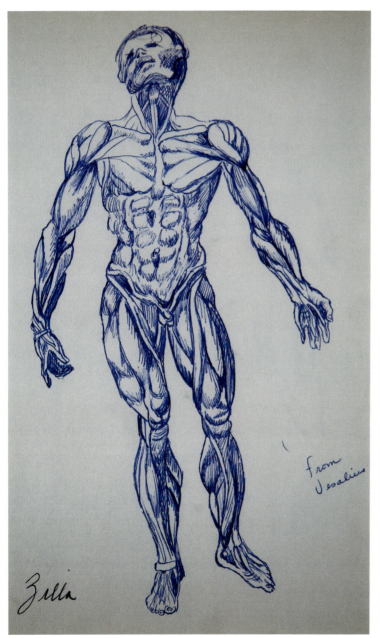
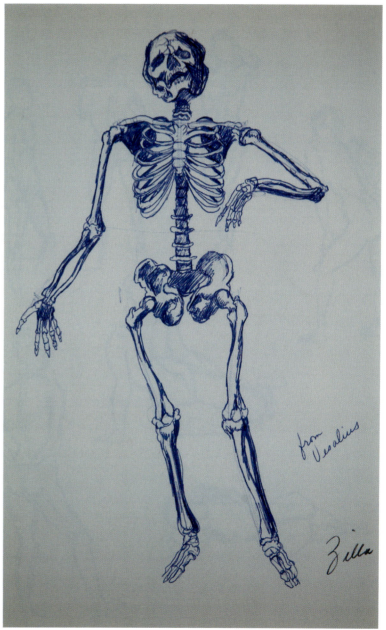

from Vesalius

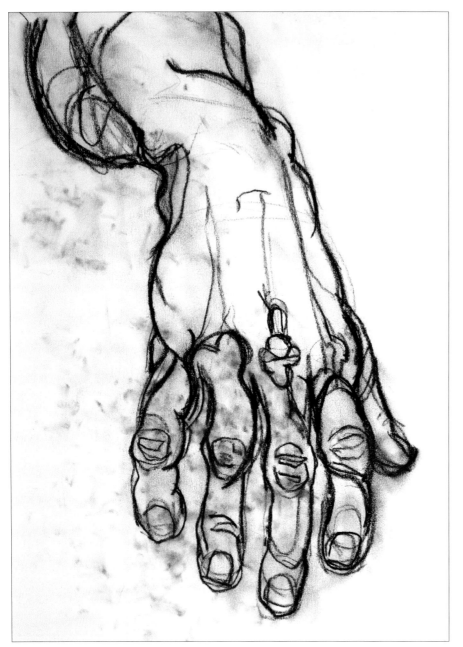
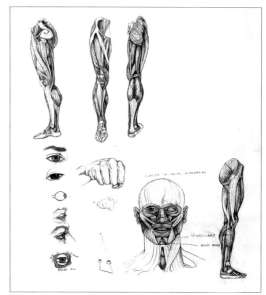
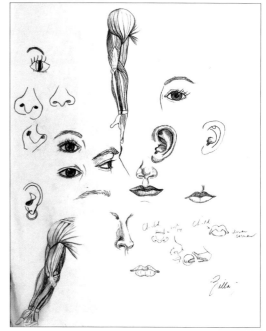

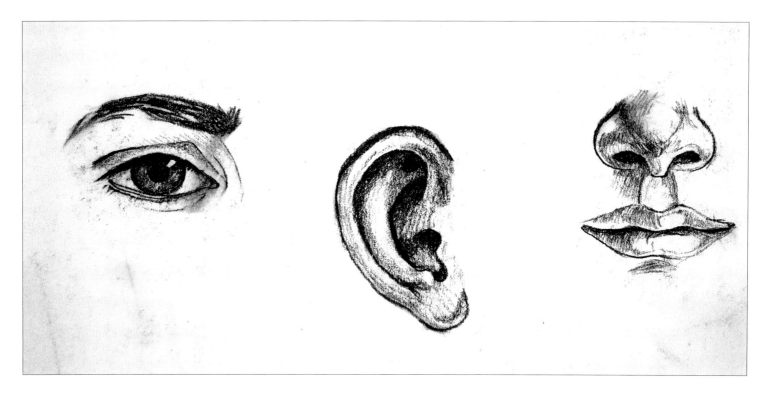

Hand (opposite, far left)
Drawn with my left hand (I'm right-handed) to increase my powers of observation and hand/brain coordination.

I did hundreds of studies in junior high school to improve my drawing ability. Practice, practice, practice!

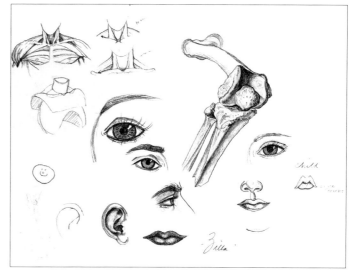

"The Model Fell Asleep"
brown conte crayon

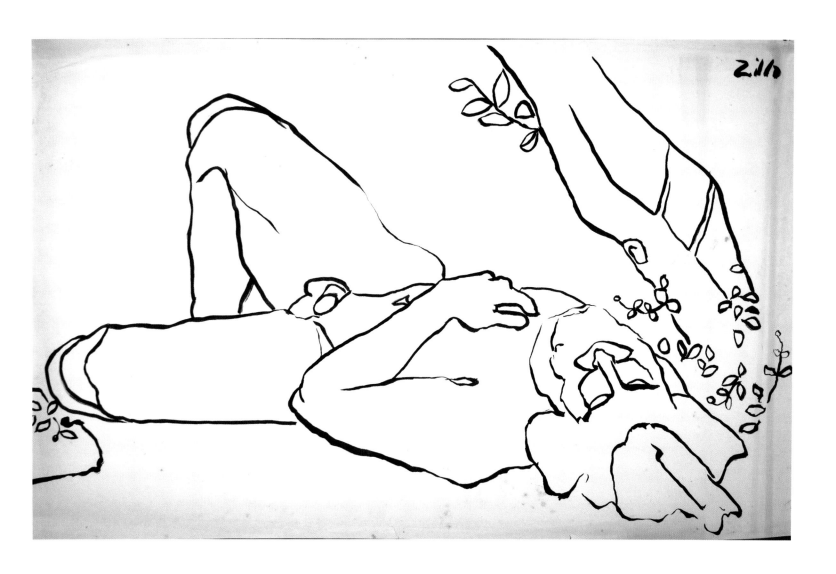

"Bearded Man Under a Tree"
I addded the tree to this studio drawing to give it more life.

"Woman with Shadow"
The shadow gives this line drawing more dimension.

"Graceful"

"Despair"

"Tammy"
This woman was my crewmate on the Machias schooner.

"Beautiful Male Proportions"

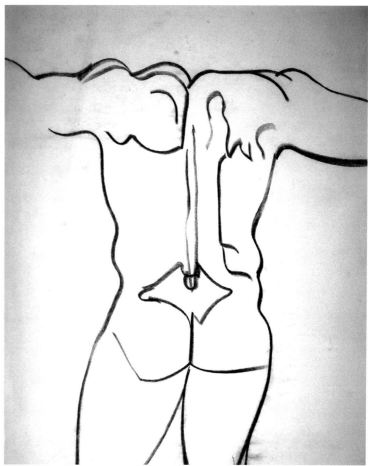

"Power and Strength"

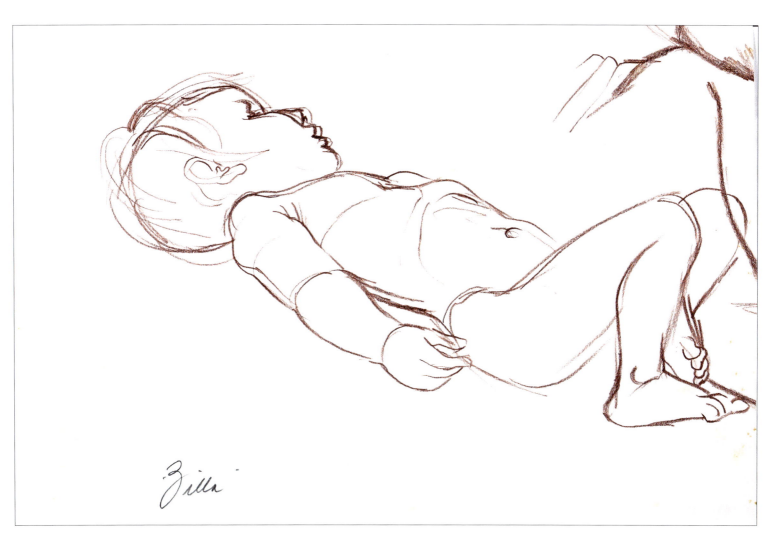

"Baby Boy Sleeping"

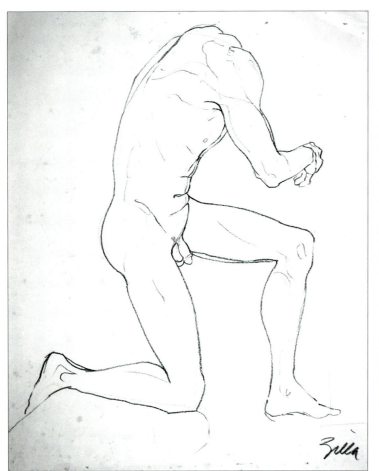

"Right Side Study"

"Maui Man"

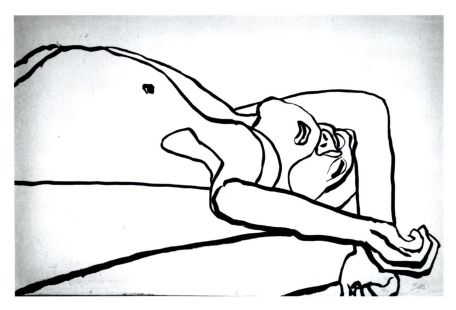

Top left: ***"A Tangle of Arms, Man Sleeping"***
Below left: ***"Contour and Light and Dark Study"***

Below right: ***"Composition with Line and Shadow"***

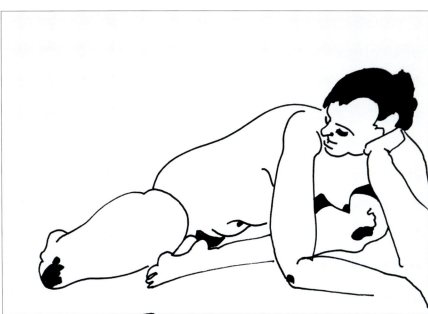

"Motion and Power"

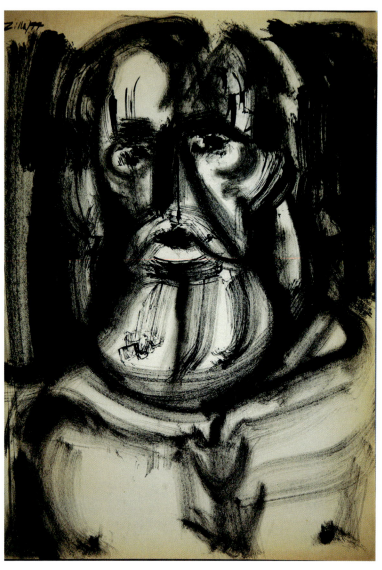

"Face of an Old Man"

"The Inferno"

"Lady on a Sofa"

"Reclining"

"A Composition of Nudes"

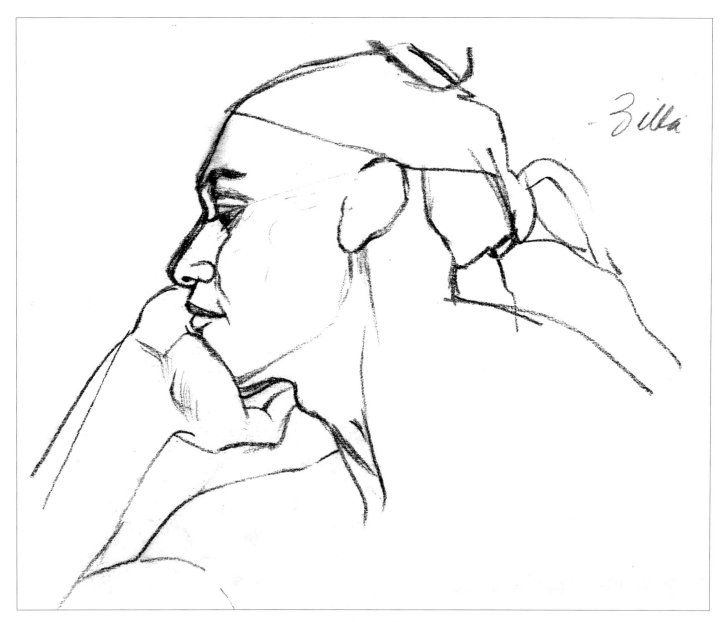

"Woman in a Turban"

"Woman on Pillows"

CHAPTER TWO

Portraits

The human face has always fascinated me. In 1963, at age 21, I presented an exhibition of 20 paintings entitled "FACES" at the University of Texas Faculty Club, The Forty Acres. I was thrilled that it was well-received at this venue.

For the portrait artist, the biggest challenge is capturing the person's expression so that it tells the story of who that person is. An accomplished portrait should convey the personality, the mood, the thoughts, and even the status and character of the individual.

In my opinion, it's one of the most difficult genres to master. I like to challenge myself by using pen and ink, which is very unforgiving, and by using as few lines as possible.

In Maui, around 1999, I was given my biggest portrait challenge. After work at the Gallery, I set up my easel on Front Street in Lahaina, the main tourist area. I planned to draw 20 minute portraits of the visitors in charcoal. At first, I felt very anxious because people would be watching me, but since one of my mottos is: "Feel the fear and do it anyway"!, I plunged ahead. To my amazement, it was really fun. My subjects came from around the world and were very interesting. Most were happy vacationers, except for the "mobster" from Chicago and his wife. I worked really nervously to make them look especially attractive!

Over the season, the hours of practice were invaluable and I developed a style that proved successful---and I even made some good money. So, if you are ever faced with a daunting art challenge, "Feel the fear and do it any way"! Your bravado will carry you through.

> *"The aim of art is to represent not the outward appearance of things, but their inward significance."*
> —ARISTOTLE
>
> *"Feel the fear and do it anyway."*
> —ZILLA ADAMS

"Self Portrait, Age 18"
Oils

"Rudy, Young Husband, Maui Street Portrait"
(20-minute drawing)

" Peggy, Young Wife, Maui Street Portrait"
This couple was on their honeymoon.

Faces of models and friends

"A Family Likeness"
Pencil drawing for a book cover I designed

"Pensive Blond"

"Carlton Kincaid"
I painted this portrait of the well-known Maui artist in 30 minutes.

"Hula Dancer, Mele"
Quick study in watercolor

"Massina"
Created for a book cover I designed

"Judgmental"

"Happy Hula Dancer"

CHAPTER THREE
Animals

Animals are wonderful subjects to draw and paint. In my painting: "At the Zoo", I was making a statement from the perspective of the birds in the cages, which are looking out at the scary people. This is opposite from our usual perspective. This was exhibited at The Texas Fine Arts Association's Annual Show at Laguna Gloria Art Museum, Austin.

I feel mixed feelings about zoos. It's wonderful to have access to the magnificent and exotic animals, and zoos may end up being the only vehicle for saving some animal species, but I feel sad that they can't be free.

Luckily many animals are available to draw from life, and I use all the same skills I use for life drawing. "The Flamingos" (page 90) were painted at the Maui Westin Hotel in Hawaii.

The tropical Hawaiian fish are utterly gorgeous, like glittering colored jewels. It's almost impossible to capture their colors in paint (pages 92, 93). The little rock squirrel drawings were done for an educational film for children, entitled: "Where Should a Squirrel Live", created by my parents, "Red" and Marjorie Adams. It won The Nature Conservancy Educational Film of the Year and The Cine Award.

I also enjoy drawing animals from my imagination and giving them anthropomorphic traits. That can be really humorous and fun.

> "Only in art will the lion lie down with the lamb and the rose grow without thorn."
> —MARTEN AMIS

"At the Zoo"

"Life Study of Flamingos"

"Clarissa the Vulture"
I like creating silly animals

"Moorish Idol"
I like to give fish and animals personalities.

"Humuhumunukunukuapuaa"
The name means "fish that oinks like a pig."
It is the state fish of Hawaii.

"Where Should a Squirrel Live"
Illustrations for a documentary film for children, which won the CINE award.

"Rocky"
My mother raised this baby squirrel then returned him to nature.

"Peace"

"Two Doves"
Linoleum block print

"The Armadillo and the Butterfly"
It makes a face.

"Big Black Bee"

CHAPTER FOUR
Florals, Plants

To me, flowers and plants are some of the most beautiful things on Earth. So I've loved drawing and painting them all my life. I was particularly inspired by the tropical plants in Key West and Hawaii. I lived in Maui for 25 years, and to my amazement, I discovered new varieties every year.

In 1989, I read a book by Barbara Ann Brennan, who was a physicist at the Goddard Space Center and a healer in Energy Medicine. In her book, *Hands of Light*, she describes being able to see the auric energy fields of plants. I was very intrigued and I followed her instructions. To my awe, I was able to *see* and *feel* their subtle energy with my hands. This changed my whole perception of a plant, shifting it from being simply a visual object of beauty, to a living being with an electromagnetic field—and perhaps even having consciousness? Humans also have electromagnetic auric fields, with which I've been working as a healer since 1986.

In my "Maui Bird of Paradise" painting, I tried to illustrate it's aqua-blue energy field, which made the painting much more special to me. My two "Banyan Tree" charcoal drawings (*page 129*) were drawn in Key West, Florida, after sailing across the Gulf of Mexico in a 36' sail boat. After so long at sea, I had missed seeing living plants and took great joy exploring their sensuous and exotic contours. That was an exciting tropical time in my life after living in Texas since my birth. The one exception was the three months I spent in Mazatlan, Mexico on vacation with my folks, and my time in Italy.

I also love to draw imaginary plants, ones that just pop into my head. I play with their design elements and create my own varieties. Why not?

> *"Put a house plant under bright lights with a dark backgound behind it. You may see lines of blue-green flashing up the plant. The aura of the leaf was a simple aqua-blue."*
>
> —BARBARA ANN BRENNAN,
> HANDS OF LIGHT

"Bird of Paradise"
I like to show the aura of the plant in my work.

"Daisies"

"Palo Alto Floral"

"Study of a Begonia"

"Flowers in a Crystal Vase"

"Oleander in a Bottle"

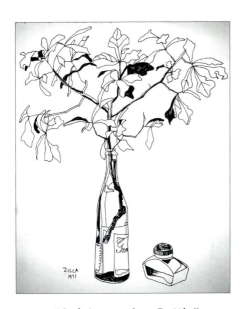

"Oak Leaves in a Bottle"

"Giant Jungle Vines"

"Tropical Beauties"
acrylic, using color harmonics to create a permanent rainbow

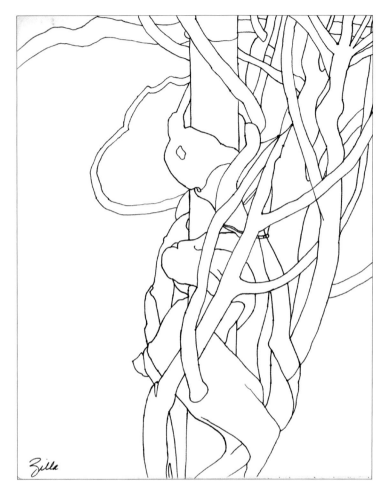

"Grape Vines I"

"Grape Vines II"

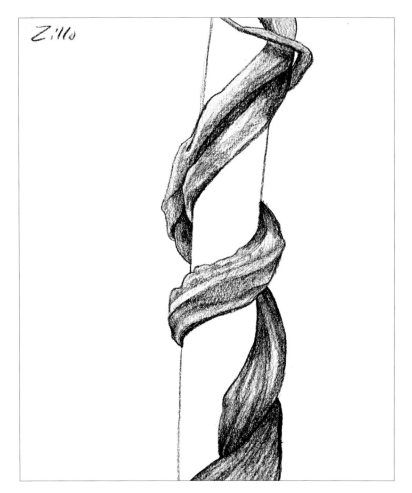

"Wysteria Vine"

"Lotus Lilly Pad"

"Spring Daisies"

"Chartreuse and Pink Floral"

"Sacred Red Ti Leaves"

"Yellow Ruffled Hibiscus"

CHAPTER FIVE
Landscapes

Even though my maternal grandmother, Wilma Davis Valentine, was a noted landscape painter, I wasn't particularly drawn to landscapes. I guess I felt that there was no way I could ever capture the extraordinary beauty of Mother Nature. Then, at age 13, my family took a vacation by car to Mazatlan, Mexico for the entire summer. It was my first introduction to the tropics and my beloved Pacific Ocean. I was literally transported, physically and emotionally, from the Texas landscape of oaks and lawns to the exotic jungles and turquoise waters of the tropics. That was the pivotal point that peeked my interest. Landscapes and seascapes became *fabulous* to me. A new genre and a new exploration began.

When I lived in Texas and Key West, I did numerous landscape drawings, which prepared me for my more serious landscape work in Hawaii.

In Maui, I chose to live in the village of Lahaina, which has been called "the Venice of the Pacific" because of the beautiful sunlight there. That's an odd coincidence because Venice is also one of my favorite cities. I fell in love with Venice in 1973.

My Maui paintings are my favorites because the colors of the mountains and ocean, and the changes in the weather are so dynamic.

I was also very impressed by the Hawaiian's deep love and respect for their land, their "aina". They have a reverence, both physical and spiritual, that guides them to be good stewards. The amazing results of this can be seen everywhere: crystal clean seas and verdant jungles, preserved. The Hawaiian Creed: "The Life of the Land is Perpetuated in Righteousness" speaks to my heart and I feel the same great love for their islands. I lived there for 25 years and I pray that they will always stay pristine and precious.

> *"The Life of the Land is Perpetuated in Righteousness."*
> —Hawaiian creed

"West Maui Mountains at Sunset"

"View of Molokai from the King's Beach I"
watercolor

"View of Molokai from the King's Beach II"
colored pencil

"Light After a Squall"

"Tropical Mountains"

"Lavender Hills"

"Old Volcanoes Resting in the Sun"

"Canoe Beach"

"The Squall is Coming"

"Gamble Gardens, Palo Alto"

"Lily Pond, California Mountains"

"Squall Over Lanai Island"

"Sugar Cane Fields in Maui II"

"Ukumehame Valley Study"

"Fishing Boats"

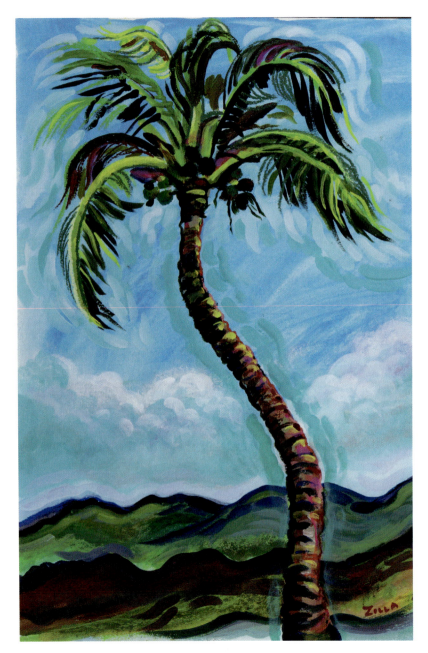

"Siblings"

"Dancing Palm"

"Banyan Tree with Orchids, Key West I"

"Banyan Tree with Orchids, Key West II"

"Big Winds, Big Waves"

"Big Sky Over Molokai"

"The Spirit of the Land"

"Sacred Rainbow at the End of Summer"

CHAPTER SIX
Collages, Mosaics

Collages have offered such variety and unexpected elements, that I really enjoy the process. I have explored every imaginable material including: foils, colored paper, newspapers, magazines, photos, cardboard, plastic, and even pieces of my old work. I've also used all media. I don't really plan a collage, I just let the work evolve as the creative surprises happen. It's more like working on a puzzle that is appearing as I work. After reviewing all my collages, I believe they are some of my best works.

I like the unpredictable compositions and diverse and unusual combinations that collage offers. My collage, "When The Rainbow Explodes", was exhibited at The Maui Cultural Center Museum in 1992. There were 700 entries in this juried show and only 70 chosen, so I consider that a good validation of my collage techniques.

In my first year at Austin High School, I began a tile mosaic (*page 17, the photo in the newspaper article*) which was my abstracted version of Paolo Uccello's painting entitled "The Battle of San Romano" (c. 1455). I was inspired by the positions of warriors and the galloping horses. My art teacher, Mrs. Jarrell, discouraged me from starting such a time consuming and difficult project. Of course, that was just the thing to spur me on.

Finally, at the end of my senior year it was finished and I took it to show her. She was really shocked! I guess I shocked myself, too, that at age 16 I had the determination to work three years on one single piece. It was a good lesson for each of us. I truly believe that if artists work hard and innovate, they can achieve great things!

Over the years, I have explored other mosaic techniques and presently my most exciting discovery is working with holographic films and holographic materials. I am combining the collage and mosaic techniques together into one unique piece.

I've always been interested in the properties of light and reflective light, and how they change as the observer moves. Using these, I have created exciting works that "magically" change colors and light properties. From different angles, they can appear brilliant or dark, painterly or reflective, all at the same time. These are my most recent explorations, which are developing into a series and a future exhibition.

> *"Learn the rules like a pro so you can break the rules like an artist."*
>
> —PABLO PICASSO

"When the Rainbow Explodes"
Mixed media in plexiglass frame

"Summer Time"

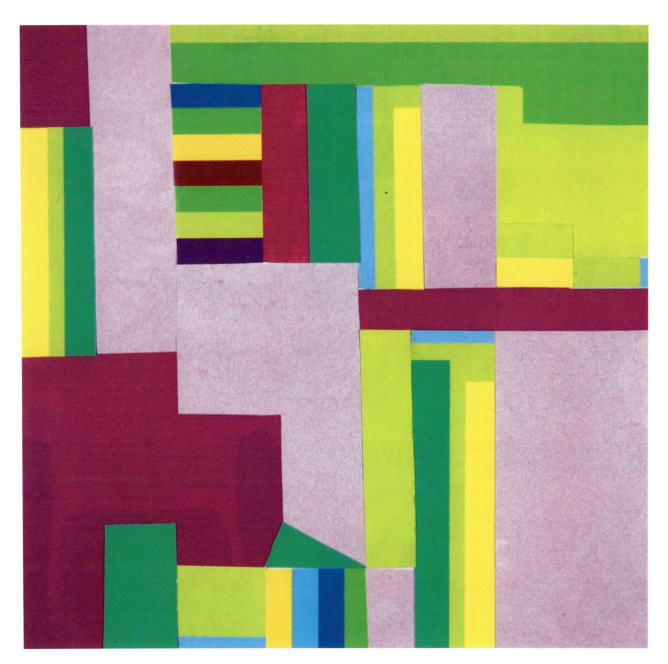

"Spring Greens and Pinks"

"Parallels"
The composition works vertically and horizontally, and even upside down.

"The Auric Spectrum of a Tropical Soul"
My energy field

"Clicks of Time"

"Traveling the Inner Map"

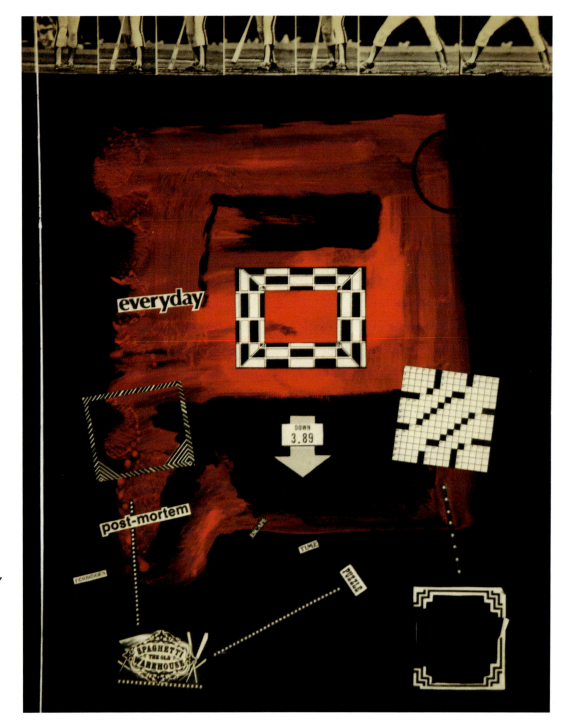

"Patterns of Life"

"The Mother Earth Goddess Creating the Seasons"

"The Encounter"

"Bamboo Forest"

"Reflections series in Green"
A collage made with holographic fabric, which reflects the light and changes colors from different vantage points.

"Reflections series in Green"
The same collage from another vantage point.

"Flight Mosaic"
One view, which shows the initial underpainting

"Flight Mosaic"
The same holographic film mosaic reflecting a different viewpoint.

"Flight Mosaic"
Another view of the refractive mosaic, showing how the film changes color from different vantage points.

"Spectral Changes"
Four views of the same holographic film mosaic, this page. Opposite, as seen from a fifth angle.

CHAPTER SEVEN

> *"The painter has the universe in his/her mind and hands."*
>
> —LEONARDO DA VINCI

I became interested in astronomy about age 11. I was shown the prism and its spectral rainbow and instantly I fell in love with light. The stars and planets were mysterious spheres that captivated my imagination. This was the beginning of my fascination with circles, the most basic form in nature. Many years later, circles reappeared in my collection of Tibetan "Thangkas", exquisite paintings of mandalas, circles representing the cosmos and enlightenment, painted with one-hair brushes in pure gold and silver paint. These prompted me to decide to travel to Kathmandu, Nepal in 2000, to see Mount Everest as my celebration of the Millennium, and to find more mandalas for my collection. This trip was the most magnificent, stunning and impactful travel experience of my life. My Nepali friends owned several galleries of Thangkas, so I joyfully added some to my collection. The majestic sight of Mount Everest brought tears of awe.

I have studied the sun, the cosmos and quantum physics for years, including the event called "Solar Max" which occurs every eleven years on the Sun. The magnetic poles totally reverse positions which causes huge solar storms and dangerous solar winds. The year 2012 was a Solar Max year, but previously, in 2009, I had begun several paintings dedicated to the Sun and the upcoming Solar Max. Of course, these paintings contained circles. It was then that I realized I had been painting circles for years. I am continuing my Solar Max series and I plan an eventual future exhibition.

In 2011, I did three monoprints of two interlocking circles at Andrea Fono's Art Studio near San Francisco. Shortly thereafter, I read that this symbol was the earliest symbol for Love, so a new series was born. However, it was put on hold until I joined Armando Rodriguez's Art Studio in Houston. He is a Master Printmaker and I share his large studio with 5 wonderful fine artists: Ilana Reisz, Maria Brown, Sally Worthington, Lind Butler, and Martha Carson. Houston has a thriving art scene and I had moved home to be near family, in the suburb of Katy, Texas. Armando's studio is a dream come true, with amazing equipment, large presses, and a massive art and music library. He has created an artistic environment that is so supportive and professional that I have plunged back into my work. My circle series has blossomed, and it is there that the idea of this book was conceived. His expertise and assistance has been a major factor in my book's creation and I feel the deepest gratitude and respect for all that he has done for me and all of us at the studio. He is the finest friend, an artistic genius, and an outstanding teacher and mentor. Gracias, Armando!!

"Solar Celebration"
Oil with colored paper collage, Solar Max series

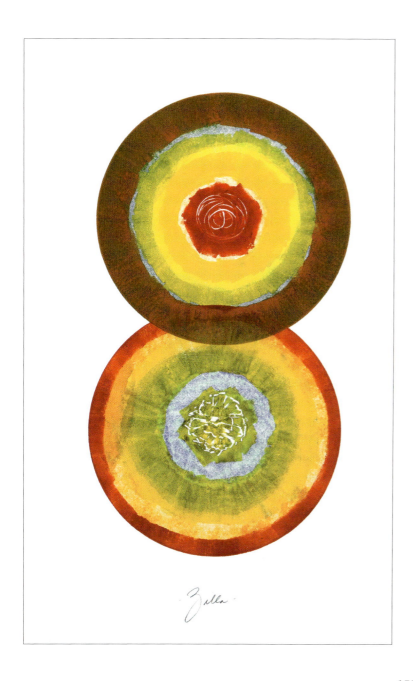

"Love: Body, Mind, and Spirit"
*A triptych of monoprints depicting conjoined circles—
the most ancient symbol for love.*

"Fiesta of Seven Circles"
monoprint

"Astral Projection"
monoprint

"Elements of the Galaxy"
monoprint, shown at the first fine art exhibition at the Johnson Space Center, NASA, Houston, Texas

"Under the Surface and Inside the Box"
acrylic painting framed in a 3D box

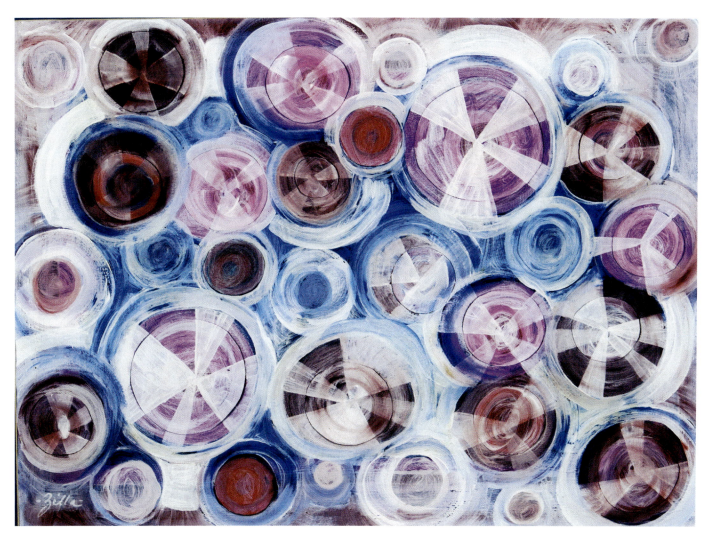

"A Cluster of Orbs (Spirits)"
mixed media collage

"The Megalithic Triple Spirals: Walking the Labyrinth to Birth"

Images taken from the spirals carved on a giant stone at the prehistoric site of New Grange, Ireland, dating from 3200 B.C. One spiral is drawn by the sun's motion every three months, so the three together total nine months, the gestation period of human birth.

The Lozenge shape represents the solar rising points of the summer and winter solstices, representing conception.

The inner magenta circle represents new life. The outer circles are fire, sun, plants, water, sea, and air.

This is an example of how I incorporate my research of ancient spiritual sites and beliefs into my art.

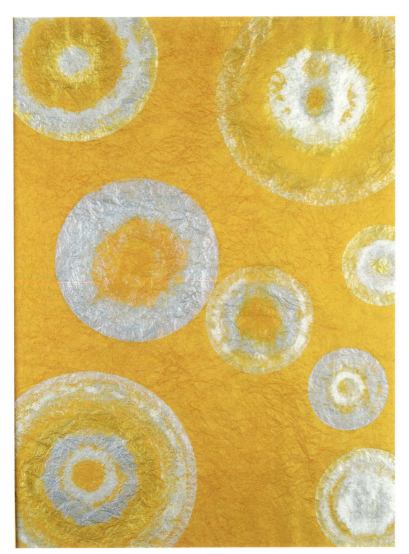

"Silver Rainbows"
monoprint on handmade paper from India

"Sun Discs"
monoprint on bronzed paper from India

"Spatial Study in Bronze"
monoprint

"Spirals Spinning"
mixed media

"The Lifegiver's Mandala"
oil painting, representing sunlight photosynthesizing a hibiscus flower

CHAPTER EIGHT
Abstracts

> *"Life is a blank canvas and you need to put all the paint on it you can."*
>
> —Danny Kaye

Throughout my life, I've been so fortunate that my mother and my grandmother were both artists, and were my visual mentors. They helped me really *look* at the world in an enhanced *observer's* manner, which few children get to experience. They taught me to SEE, rather than LOOK.

My Mom and I would be driving at dusk and she would say: "See how lavender the highway looks!" Lavender? Roads are not lavender! Then I would actually *see* the lavender tone that the light had created on the road! WOW! This blew the windows of my visual mind wide open! I instantly had a whole new way of perceiving the world!

This sort of lesson came from my Grandmother, too, as she pointed to a Chinese Tallow Tree and said, "Look, that tree has yellow, orange, red and burgundy leaves and it's trunk is very grey". It was true! I saw it! Trees are not just green and brown. I was being taught to really SEE!

Over the years, I have passed-on this precious art of SEEING to my children and my grandchildren because I have wanted their lives to be as visually enriched as mine was.

Being able to SEE is primary for an artist's development. Vincent Van Gogh, Paul Gauguin and the Fauves are examples of taking this ability to extremes. When they saw color, they dialed-it-up, creating even richer and more exciting colors in their works. Thus, the world SAW in a new way, too.

After teaching in elementary schools, I have felt really sad that so many children do not get visual training, especially since a huge percentage of learning comes from sight.

Yet, the schools hardly focus on it. I believe that children are capable of understanding all the elements of good composition, and of abstract art. At a very early age, I was exposed to classical music, dance, theater, good poetry, and literature, and I believe that cultural awareness and good taste can be taught. A person needs a certain level of training before they can truly appreciate all the elements of an art work. These elements include: color harmonics, perspective, texture, light and dark contrast, line quality, patterns and rhythms, the finesse of the gesture, the mood it evokes, and the communication the observer receives. I believe all these can be taught to a young child.

When I was in Paris, at the Centre Georges Pompidou Art Museum, I witnessed a little French girl, about nine years old, discussing an abstract painting with her mother.

Since I speak basic French, I heard her analyzing these different aspects of composition, so happily and enthusiastically, that it was a joy for me to experience. At that moment, I dearly wished that all American children could have such a thrill. Art truly feeds the soul.

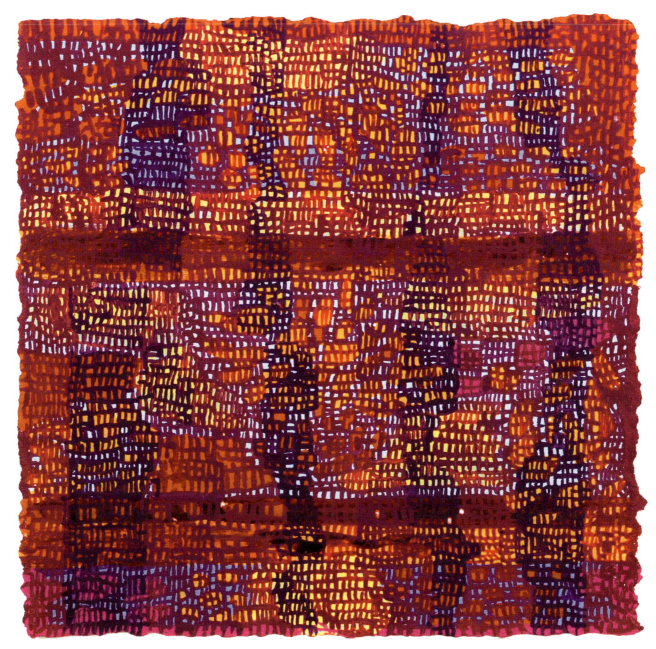

"The Weave of Life"
acryic, with gold paint

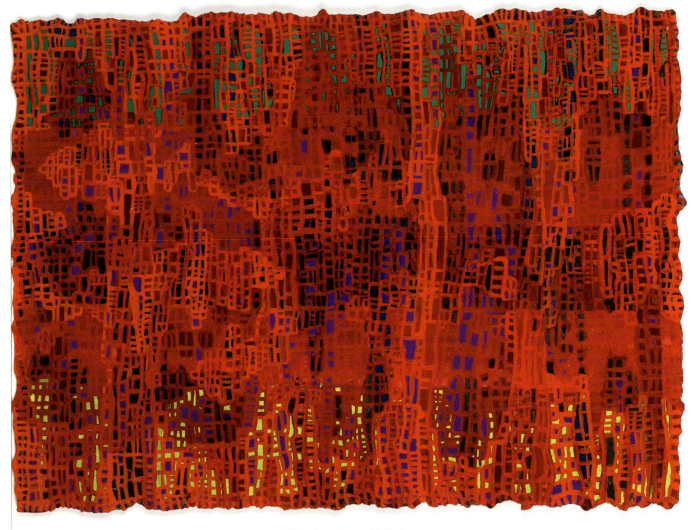

"The Passion of Life"
acrylic

"The Path of Life"
acrylic

"Playing with Angles"
acrylic

"Backed Into Both Corners"
acrylic

"The Stab"
acrylic

"Messages Coming Through"
mixed media, pewter paint

"The Genius"
oil painting

"The Shrine to the Aina (Earth)"
at right: assemblage, semi-prcious stones, wire, oil

Exhibited at the Maui International Goddess Conference, Hawaii

Veiwers are encouraged to touch the painting as they say a prayer for the Earth.

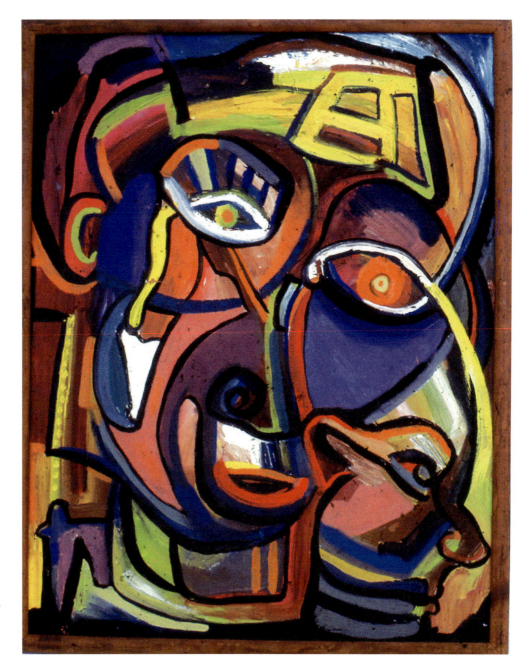

"Eyes on You"
oil painting

"Cubistic Portrait of Joe"
oil painting

"Hurricane"
silver, metallic acrylics

"Flurry"
acrylic

"Festival of Evil"
acrylic

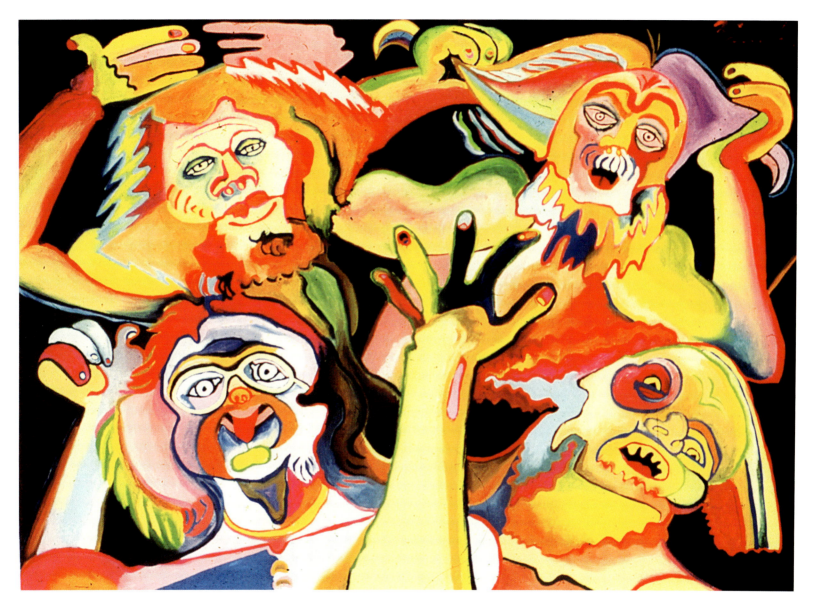

"The Asylum"
oil painting
This was first exhibited at the Fine Arts Museum at the University of Texas, Austin

"Memories and Tributes to Our Artist Ancestors"
oil painting, Inspired after viewing the preshistoric cave paintings of southern France

"Spirit Cave Animals"
acrylic collage

In 2009, after studying the 35,000 year-old Prehistoric art in 14 ancient caves in southern France, I was inspired to paint my deeply spiritual experiene in three paintings.

"Zilla in the Cave Witnessing the Return of the Venus of the Sacred Feminine"
oil painting

CHAPTER NINE
Etchings

> *"The artist is nothing without the gift, but the gift is nothing without the work."* —EMILE ZOLA

I found Etching (intaglio) to be a hard taskmaster. It was time-consuming, and required patience, diligence and discipline to be successfully executed. Happily, all of these paid off when my etching entitled: "The Cry" was exhibited at the University of Texas Art Museum, at the Perry Casteneda Library. John Canady, the famous art critic for *The New York Times,* was one of the Jurors of that show. Luckily, I got to meet him at the opening party and that was very exciting!

"The Cry" needs an explanation: a Native American Indian face (mask) is in the background and it is crying six large tears, which represent some of the Western influences that over took and decimated their culture. These influences are illustrated inside each tear. From left to right they are: western music, the atomic age, science, western thought and philosophy with Voltaire's portrait, the mechanical water pump, western religion with the figures of Adam and Eve, and in the tear between the mask's eyes, the loss of their buffalo. This final blow caused starvation and the ultimate demise of their civilization. I have always had the deepest compassion for our Native Americans and the loss of their eons of knowledge and wisdom. I created this work as an homage to them and in recognition of their suffering.

Etching techniques also allowed me to play with reverse images, as in the "The Horse" and "Face of Thinking Man". They are two printed images of the same work, one printed upside-down.

My "Icarus" etching has so many subtleties that it has photographed very dark. Icarus is ready to fly to the Sun, seen as two orbs above him, which represent his two flaws, vanity and hubris. The ball in the lower right corner is what is left of the melted Icarus, just a swirling ball with matter flying off of it. This represents his downfall. There is a hint of the larger Sun behind him, which is larger than he is.

The surreal object that is giving off light in "Light Flower" is an imaginary creation. I think it would be wonderful if flowers could create light. This etching was difficult because the mezzotint got progressively fainter and darker, which was hard to achieve.

"The Cry, the Demise of the American Indian Culture by the West"
etching

"Face of Thinking Man"
etching
Same plate showing a different image (opposite), when the print is turned upside-*down.*

"Face of Horse"
etching

"Icarus"
etching

"Light Flower"
etching

CHAPTER TEN

Sculptures

In 1973, I studied sculpture with the noted sculptor, Charles Umlauf. This was a dream come true. I completed two standing figures, one female and one male (*pages 192, 193*), which were cast in hydrastone (marble dust), and finished with a "bronze" patina. They made an interesting pair because the female was slender, delicate and demure, and the male was muscular, strong and proud, with his hands on his hips. These were so successful, that I wanted to create a more complex subject.

I wanted a male figure who was straining under a weight of some kind, which would make the anatomy more dynamic. I also considered the possibilities of an old man. I finally decided to combine the two into one piece. The young man could be active, muscular and powerful, and the old man could be passive, emaciated and weak. I was quite excited, but I had no access to a male model, so I had to rely on anatomy books. I planned to position the old man on the young man's shoulders, for a heavier burden.

The symbolic possibilities were numerous. The element of TIME could be introduced by having the old man represent the young man's future, and the young man could be the old

man's past. Linked together physically, they could be the same person at different stages in life. To achieve this, I designed the old man's beard to flow into the young man's hair, and their hands to be holding onto each other. The old man represents old age and ultimate death, which is the final burden that all humans carry. Thus, I chose the name, "Burdens". These ideas were promising, but it was the surprise that I had in Europe, later that year, that cemented my plans.

In May, 1973, during my fifth month of my third pregnancy,

I left for Europe with my University of Texas "Renaissance Art History" class. My husband, Joe, and I had been saving funds for a year and the initial deposit for this trip had been paid. I was finally getting my trip to Europe that Joe had promised when we got engaged 10 years ago.

I had agreed to put him through Law School, if he sent me to study art in Europe. I was going to get full credit for a class in only six weeks. Then came the big surprise: I was expecting our third baby! After much debate, my Doctor gave me permission to travel, and so the trip was still on! What a beautiful gift...actually, two beautiful gifts!

Our professor, Dr. McDonald Smith, PhD. was the top expert on Renaissance Art History, so I was ecstatic! However, it was hard to leave my little ones, daughter, Kelly, and son, Adam, for so long. But, they got the great opportunity to go to Country Day Camp all day, so they were thrilled! So, it all worked out in the end. The course covered the entire Renaissance as it moved from Italy in 1200, across Europe, to England in the 18th century. It was a most comprehensive course, which included the art in nine countries. My 2nd big surprise occurred in Rome as our class was touring the Vatican Palace. We saw a huge fresco by the Master, Raphael, c.1513, and the subject was "Aeneas Carrying His Father, Anchises From The Burning Ruins of Troy". Old Anchises was being carried "piggyback" on his son, Aeneas's, back! Seeing this subject, which was so similar to my own idea, really impacted me and validated my sculpture! My decision to create it was made!

I worked for four months on "Burdens" (pages 194, 195). I cast it in hydrastone and hydracal, and added a final "bronze" patina. I felt this accomplishment really meant something! The trip and the sculpture were big highlights in my life!

About two months later, another big highlight in my life arrived on September 17th, the birth of Alethea Katherine Witherspoon,

> *"Proportion is the heart of beauty."*
> —KEN FOLLET

our beautiful and precious daughter! She was my most incredible creation in 1973! Evidently she had also thrived on this trip! She was perfect

I didn't have the opportunity to do another sculpture until 1991. At that time, I had lived in Lahaina, Maui for four years, in a large beach house with a studio, and I was doing well at my job at The Village Gallery. My daughter, Kelly, had lived with me there for a year, and my son, Adam, was there attending college and enjoying the surfing.

In Hawaii, rainbows are seen almost every day. These beauties gave me the idea of doing a "light-flight" sculptural piece which would hang from a ceiling and produce a rainbow. If I designed it properly, the colors would reflect off the surface naturally. I didn't want to use colored paint. I wanted my rainbow to be created with the properties of light, itself. I chose white plexiglass for the sculpture. I knew that when direct light hits a color, the reflected light would be the same color. So, a rainbow could be made to reflect on the white shiny surface. I could create colored light *without* electricity.

I built a model with white foam core and I experimented... and it worked! So I had the enlarged piece made in plexiglass. It was an imposing six feet across! To my delight, "Light Flight" (*page 193*) was accepted in the big Annul Jury Show, "ART MAUI, 1991"! My six months of work paid off. The Juror, Richard Nelson, the art teacher from Yale, said to me, "This is the most sophisticated sculptural concept I've ever seen". That was overheard by several at the show, so that was quite a compliment! I hope to continue sculpting for many years, as it is one of the most demanding genres, and I love the challenges of 3D!

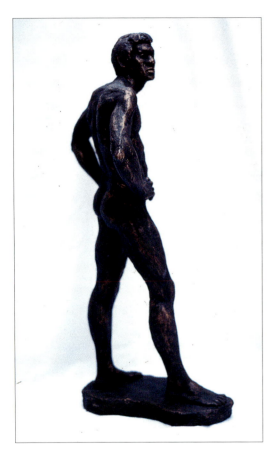 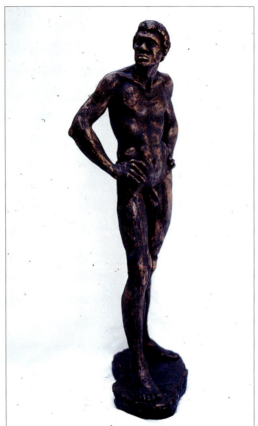 

"Attitude"
cast hydrastone, showing three different views of the sculpture

"Light Flight"
*suspended plexiglass sculpture,
creating a reflected rainbow
without electricity*

"Woman"
terracotta, uncast version

"Burdens"
*cast hydrastone, showing different
views of the sculpture*

CHAPTER ELEVEN

Pen and Ink, Surrealism

I have always loved to draw. I often pick up a pen and tablet and begin, just to see what pops up. It is really more like "channeling" or automatic writing. I don't plan it, nor control it, nor restrict it, nor judge it. A subject will quickly begin to manifest, as I am an "artist/adventurer" exploring the unknown. I'm "examining life" just as Socrate's quote instructed me to do when I was twelve.

When I was young, my Mother couldn't keep enough paper in our house. I drew constantly, so to keep up with the demand, she became one of the first recyclers long before anyone had heard that term. She trimmed used papers and made them re- usable for me. When I think back on that, I have to laugh. Actually, both my parents were tremendously supportive and respectful and helped me realize my dreams.

As for my subjects, faces have appeared repeatedly through out my life. Some are funny, some are scary, some are whimsical, or weird or surreal. Sometimes, I like to anthropomorphize (give human traits) to intangible things, like the Wind, or Mother Nature, or Jack Frost, or Madusa, even Death. Sometimes, I have used these drawings for serious paintings, such as "The Genius" (*page 174*).

I have loved faces so much that, over the years, I've collected 145 masks from all over the world. When I moved onto the sailboat, I had to cull them. At present, I still have about 45, which are my favorites. Faces aren't my only favorite subjects. I like funny animals, dragons, and unusual, weird and surreal images. I think they are some of my most original works...and the most fun. Awhile back, I read: " Don't be scared to be open-minded, your brain isn't going to fall out". I keep this in mind when I draw. There is another quote that I love by Jean Cocteau: "Art is the marriage of the conscious and the unconscious."

Art can express anything, and for me anything goes! I particularly love to draw things that make me laugh out loud. I explore any subject, and animals can be quite

> *"The position of the artist is humble. She is essentially a channel."*
> —PIET MONDRIAN

FACES

"Frilly"

funny, as is poor "Clarissa, The Vulture", who is ""nature's charwoman" (*page 91*).

Art is my entertainment, my mouth-piece, my escape, my solace, my therapy, my social commentary, my fun, my joy. I use it to express beauty, to intellectualize, to keep memories, to joke, to be original, silly and surreal. As I let my imagination fly, I try to illustrate impossible or incomprehensible things, such as gravity, electric energy, magnetic fields or elements of Quantum Physics which are inconceivably small. I love philosophy and studying the various religions and ethnic beliefs. I've traveled to 26 countries and love indigenous art, which I've collected. I have developed my own spiritual beliefs, which I have illustrated in my own way. I've even painted my rarest experience of going into the prehistoric caves in France, and my awe at seeing art that is 35,000 years old! It was one of the most stunning, and cherished experiences of my life!

The most precious thing for me as an artist is having an open mind, and having the freedom of expression in a free country, where my rights as an artist and as a woman are guaranteed and protected. Without these, art would be a sham and a false pursuit, so, right here and now, I declare my deepest gratitude for the fact that I am free!

"Wired"

"Bad Hair Day"

"A Faun or Satyr of Sorts"

"Earnestness"

"Man with Glasses"

"Disbelief"

"Old Man"

"Pele, The Volcano Goddess

"Leaf Lady"

"The Professor"

"Frizzie"

"Hey, Baby"

"The Spiral Goddess"

"Nature Never Sleeps"

"Aristocrat"

"Thoughts Broadcasting"

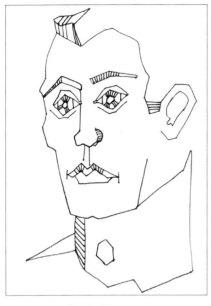

"Blinded by Love"

"Sea Nymph"

"Mackenzie"

"Delight"

"Can You Trust Me?"

"Inside and Outside"

"You're So Vain"

"Prima Vera"

"Man with a Mustache"

"Sophia Loren"

"Painted Mask"

"Patterned Profile"

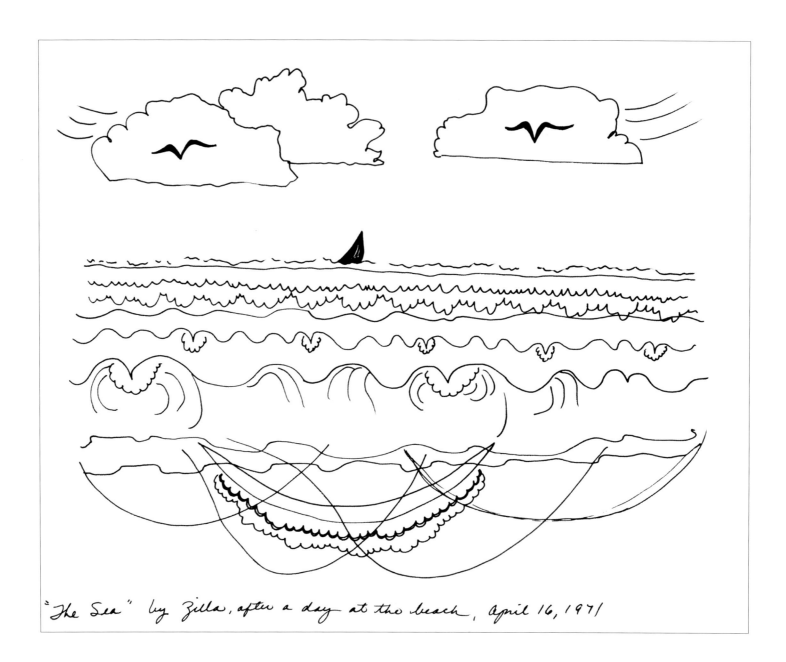

SURREALISM

"The Scream"

"The Time Machine"

"The Iliad's Homer"

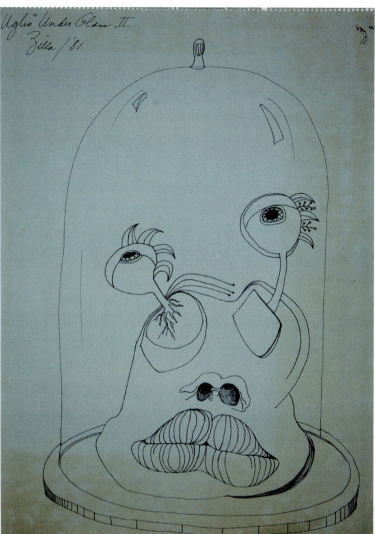

"Reverse Drapery" "An Uglio Under Glass"

— 211 —

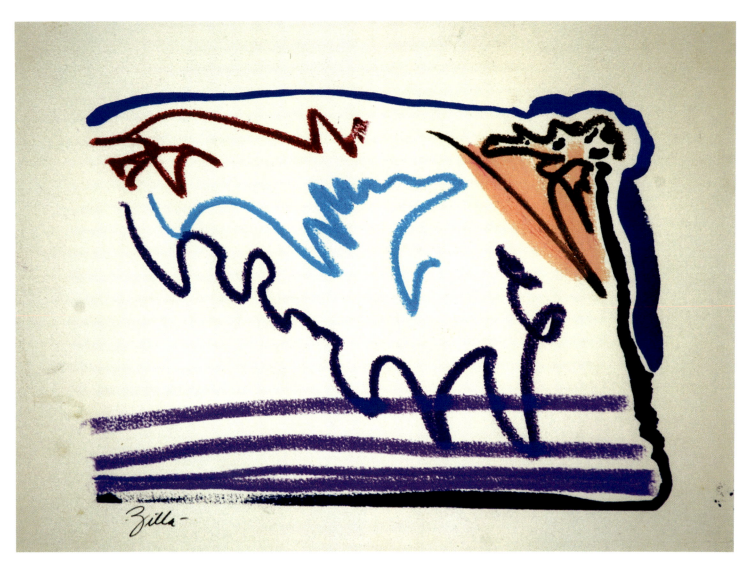

"Approaching Storm"
crayon

"Red Rover"
crayon

"Sad Jester"

"Dog Lady"

"Cubism Waving at Picasso"

"Mother Nature"

"Fighting Dragon"

"Germination"

"Mother Nature's Jewels"

"Menacing"

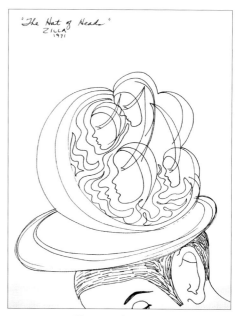

"A Hat of Heads"

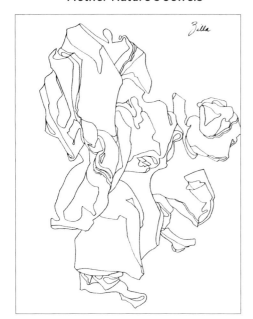

"Clean Clothes, Dancing"

"The Rain Walking In"

— 215 —

"Call Me"

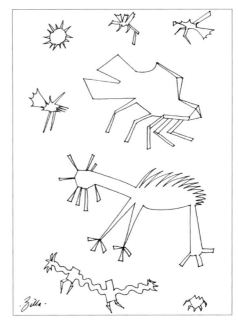

"Imaginary Amimals"

"You Are Only As Extinct as You Think You Are"

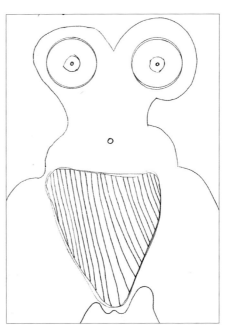

"Danger Zone I"

"Two LInes Gossiping"

"Prayers for the Children of Haiti"

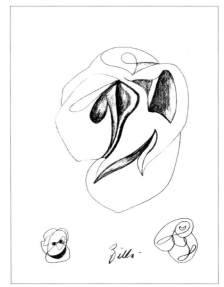
"Design for a Sculpture"

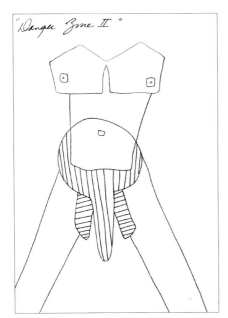
"Danger Zone II"

"War Bonnet"

"Spring Time"

"Dreamscape II"

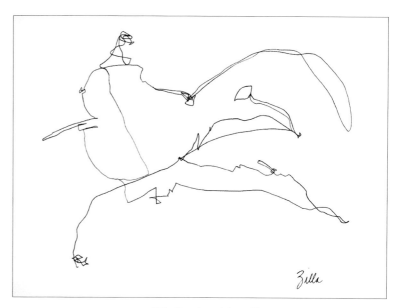
"Galloping Lines"

"Systems and Dimensions"

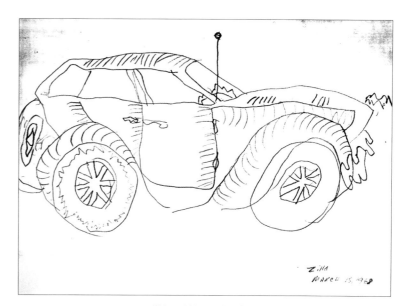
"Key West Cruiser"

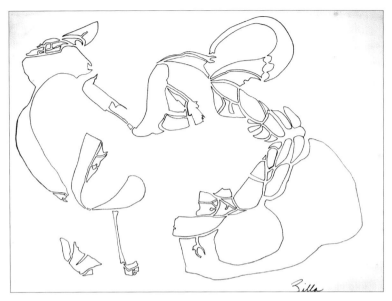

"Images Morphing"

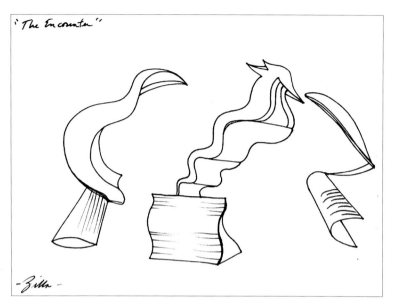

"The Encounter"

"Terra Femme"

*"Earth Being Sucked Into
A Black Hole"*

"Figurative Symbols"

"The Cosmic Noisemaker"

"Dancing Slants and Folds"

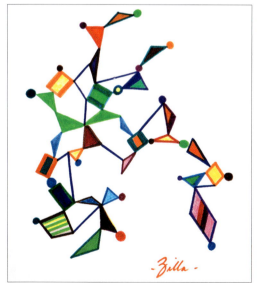

"Connect the Dots"

"Architectural Geometry"

"The Big Question"

| CHAPTER TWELVE |

Drawing my Story

I was married to Joe in 1963, so I had been a wife for seven years when the 1970's "hit". At that time, our daughter, Kelly, was five years old and our son, Adam, was one.

Today, few people realize how different a woman's life was before 1970, unless they actually lived through it. Prior to 1970, it was a man's world, with men having all the legal powers. A woman could not get a loan without her husband's permission, nor could she have a credit card in her name. A pregnant woman could not work. There were no laws protecting a woman in the work place, even if she experienced sexual harassment. There were no child-support laws insuring that fathers had to support their children. Colleges had quotas which prevented women from entering professional fields like medicine or law. The Ivy League schools were all males only. Even in sports, there were no scholarships for female students. Women were not equal under the law. Then came The Women's Liberation Movement and everything changed. Women became informed and realized they could create options if they organized. Thousands marched in huge demonstrations, creating a massive cultural movement. The NOW (National Organization of Women) was formed, and Gloria Steinem published "MS" Magazine.

> *"Life is change, growth is optional, choose wisely."*
> —UNKNOWN

The "Battle of the Sexes" exploded and a huge social shift began, effecting women's roles, and men's, too.

Many women questioned who they were and what their lives meant. The roles of wife and mother were no longer enough, nor as valued as before. It created a crisis coming from the outside. Women were expected to carry on, and become professionals in midstream. As a wife and mother, and an artist, I felt immense pressure. And I was not alone. I went back to college to finish my degree, which I had chosen to postpone to help put my new husband through law school. It was much more difficult with three children, since our baby daughter, Alethea, had been born. I juggled my family's needs and study time, which was usually after the children were in bed. Finally, in 1979, I got my Bachelors Degree in Fine Art from the University of Texas. I felt great pride in the fact that I could now help support my family, if necessary.

There were many casualties as a result of these massive changes. Marriages underwent extreme stresses. Divorce became rampant because marriages simply could not adjust. Every couple we knew was struggling or divorced. Our own divorce was devastating, especially to our children, our precious innocents.

Simultaneously, there was the crisis from the inside: The Mid-Life Crisis. A term which tried to explain the additional inner turmoil that hits people in their mid-thirties. Unfortunately, there were no new rules, no new guidelines to follow to deal with all these serious issues. The fabric of our lives was torn asunder, with no help in sight.

Additionally, I had several serious health issues to handle. Fortunately, my "cancer scares" were successfully eliminated by surgeries, and I bounced back every time. However, any confrontation with cancer and "possible" death, was extremely terrifying! During this period, I did several drawings about "Death", as my way of dealing with it.

In every life, there is some pain to endure. As an artist, my drawings gave me solace and helped my express and process that pain. Life is full of lessons and our job is to learn and transcend. We must choose how we handle the tragedies in our lives. Hopefully, we gain understanding of ourselves and others, and rise above, as we evolve spiritually. Life keeps moving on, and hopefully, time heals all wounds. I have sought forgiveness, realizing it to be the most powerful spiritual, healing tool in life.

In my last drawing (*page 231*), I quote myself:

All the different experiences in my life may be nothing more than opportunities to learn how to give and receive love. And the sole purpose of life itself may be to become a truly loving being.

Blessings to all my dearly beloveds!

Above: Grandmother Wilma Valentine's oil painting, **"Texas shack"**

A sketch of the first painting that I sold. I was 14 years old. **"Grief"**

Sketch of Zilla by Jim Caulthron, a classmate at UT

Below: Children: Kelly and Adam, recovering from their accident, which is why they look so sad. Ali, at right, at 2 1/2 years old.

Sketch of my father when he was 56

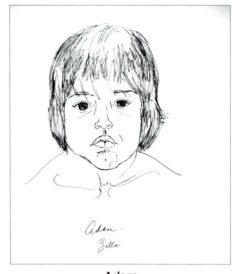

Kelly **Adam** **Ali**

Joe Witherspoon, our first year of marriage

Living room of the Villa de Zilla, with Ali sitting on the bench

"The Mermaid Is Shocked at the Way Things Are"

"Warhorse"

"Blood Bath"

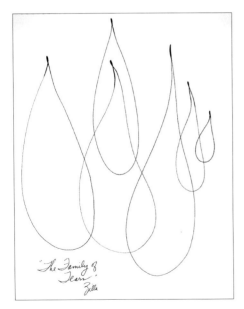

"A Family of Tears"

"Waiting Out the Storm"

"The Dragon Standing Her Ground"

"My Path, How Smooth Will It Be?"

"Study, John Doonan"

"Study, Countess Evelyn Lambert"

"Mayday / Le Mariage"

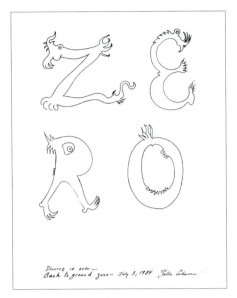
"Divorce is Over, So Back to Ground Zero"

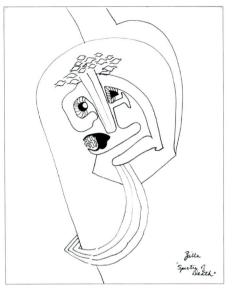
"Spector of Death"

"Death is Laughing"

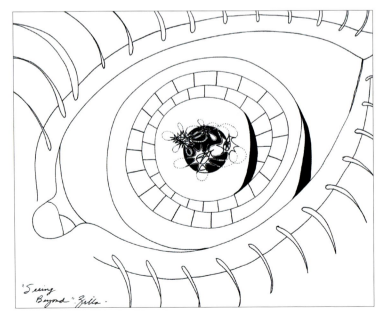
"Seeing Beyond"

"Transformation and Healing"

All the different experiences in life may be nothing more than opportunities to learn how to give and recieve love....

And the sole purpose of life itself may be to become a truly loving being...

Zilla

Biographical Information

Zilla Adams, Fine Artist

PROFESSIONAL HISTORY

Born May 6, 1942, in Austin, Texas, USA
Began drawing recognizable subjects at age 20 months; and at 2 ½ years of age announced, "I am an artist."

EDUCATION

WOOLDRIDGE ELEMENTARY SCHOOL, Austin, Texas
• At age 11, was accepted as the youngest member of the University of Texas "Gifted and Talented Junior Art Project," studying painting and life drawing with UT professors for 3 years.

O. HENRY JUNIOR HIGH SCHOOL, Austin, Texas
• At age 13, studied life drawing at the Laguna Gloria Art Museum School, Austin.
• In 1956, at age 14, Zilla sold her first painting, entitled "Grief."
• Accepted into her First Jury Show, Texas University's "Junior Art Project" Children's Exhibition.

S. F. AUSTIN HIGH SCHOOL, Austin, Texas
• At age 15, produced artwork for *The Maroon*, the school newspaper.
• Director of the school's annual Christmas decoration contest.
• At age 16, her artwork was chosen for display at the annual State of Texas Teacher's Convention in Dallas.
• Elected secretary of the Paint and Palette Art Club.
• At age 17, elected president of the Paint and Palette Art Club.
• Chairman of the school's "Deck The Doors" contest.
• Exhibited a painting at The Laguna Gloria Art Museum's Annual "Fiesta."
• Exhibited an oil painting at the Wellesley Junior Art Exhibit.
• Graduated from S.F. Austin High School in 1960, in the top quarter of her class.

THE UNIVERSITY OF TEXAS, Austin, Texas
• Majored in applied art (studio, with a minor in art history), Bachelor of Fine Art degree plan
• Art Student's Association member, 1960 through 1963.
• Three drawings displayed at the UT Fine Art building.
• 1961, elected art supervisor of Alpha Gamma Delta sorority, 1961-1963.
• Three paintings exhibited in the UT Student Exhibition, Regent's Room.
• 1961, age 19, First Solo Exhibition at Ford Paint Company, featuring 25 works in oil, casein, and watercolor.
• 1962, age 20, Second Solo Exhibition at Alpha Gamma Delta sorority, with cover story in Alpha Gamma Delta's *National Magazine*.
• KASE radio interview, "Community Show Case" program.
• KTBC radio interview, "Jack Wallace and Jim Cummings Show."
• UT Varsity Carnival entry winner for Alpha Gamma Delta Sorority, "The Queenship for Concessions" award.
• 1963, age 21, UT Campus Art Competition, three Citation Awards. Juried by the faculty of the UT art department.
• Television interview (20 minutes) for KLRN, the Educational TV station, operated by UT.
• Third Solo Exhibition at the Villa Capri, Austin, Texas. 25 works in mixed media.
• Age 21, Fourth Solo Exhibition at The Forty Acres UT Faculty Club, Austin, Texas. "Faces, Variations on a Theme."
• Exhibited a mosaic, "The Battle," in the Goodfriend's Exhibition, Austin, Texas.
• 1963, met and married Joseph Parker Witherspoon III in Austin, Texas. In 1964, moved to Houston for Joe's job as Assistant District Attorney for Harris County.
• 1965, daughter, Kelly Valentine Witherspoon, born in Houston, Texas.

THE UNIVERSITY OF HOUSTON, Houston, Texas
• 1966, age 24, resumed studies, bachelor of fine art degree. Studied sculpture at the Houston Museum Fine Art School, with David Parsons, professor of art, Rice University.
• 1967, studied life drawing with William Hoey at the Houston Museum of Fine Art School.

- Life Drawings exhibited at the Student's Art Exhibition, Houston Museum of Fine Art.
- 1968, organized the Children's Art Show at the University of Houston's Laboratory Nursery School, Home Economics Department.
- 1969, son, Adam Joseph Witherspoon, born in Houston, Texas.
- 1970, "Reclining Nude," a cast aluminum sculpture, exhibited at the University of Houston Student Center.
- Studied Life Drawing at the Houston Art League, evening workshop, Houston, Texas.
- Exhibited in the New Members Exhibition, Houston Art League, Houston, Texas.
- 1972, exhibited drawing, "The Dog of Time," The Texas Fine Arts Association Region One Citation Show, Elisabet Ney Art Museum, Austin, Texas.

THE UNIVERSITY OF TEXAS, Austin, Texas
- 1973, Joe and Zilla, age 31, moved their family back to Austin and Zilla resumed her bachelors degree program.
- 1973, studied abroad with UT Art History Tour in Europe. Six weeks in nine European countries, "Renaissance Art History" taught by Dr. MacDonald Smith, Phd., professor of art history.
- 1973, daughter, Alethea Katherine Witherspoon, was born in Houston, Texas.
- 1976, studied life drawing with Bill Hollaway at the Elisabet Ney Museum School, in Austin.
- 1977, shared a two-person exhibition, with artist Mary Helen McFarlane, titled "Black and White." Upstairs Gallery, Bradford Paint Company. A total of 60 works, including drawings, paintings, and prints in black and white.
- Exhibited two paintings at the Seguin Art Center Painting and Sculpture Exhibition: "Life is a Puzzle" and "Ghosts in the Garden." Juried by John Evett and Lawrence D. Miller III, curator of the Austin Contemporary Art Museum.
- 1977, at age 35, resumed bachelors degree studies, UT.
- Life drawing entitled "The Old Man" was chosen for display in the UT art building by Professor Robert Levers, chairman of the art department exhibition committee.
- 1978, exhibited a large oil painting, 36" x 40", entitled "The Asylum" at the Texas Fine Arts Association, Region I State Citation Show. The Elisabet Ney Art Museum, Austin, Texas, Juror: Robert Levers.
- Zilla was one of the Founders of The Austin Contemporary Visual Arts Association.
- Exhibited two acrylic paintings: "Aurora's Dance," 18"x 24", and "Helios" 18"x 24" at the Austin Contemporary Visual Arts Association's First Juried Exhibition, held at St. Edwards University, Mary Moody Hall, Austin, Texas. Juror: Stan Irwin.
- 1978, Fifth Solo Show at Beverly Hayden's Gallery, Austin, Texas.
- 1978, pen and ink drawing entitled: "Zilla's House" was chosen by UT instructor, Susan Whyne, for display at the UT art building.
- Etching entitled: "The Cry" included in the UT Annual Student Art Auction at The Castenada Library. Jury comprised of Fredericka Hunter, owner of Texas Gallery, Houston; Robert Murdoch, Curator of Contemporary Art at the Dallas Museum of Fine Art; and John Canady, former Art Critic for the *New York Times*.
- Acrylic painting: "Frost," chosen by Professor Bill Wyman for display at the UT art building.
- 39th Annual Art Student's Exhibition, two paintings: "The Genius," and "When All Else Fails," exhibited at the Huntington Gallery of the UT Fine Art Museum.
- Term paper on Mayan Art History entitled: "An Iconographic Study and Comparison of Two Carved Maya Monuments, Stela 30 From Naranjo and Stela 10 from Seibal," co-authored by Sharon Gill and Amy Nash, with illustrations by Zilla, was included in the Latin American Collection Library at UT on the request of Professor Linda Schele, Phd. An additional copy was placed at the University of South Alabama by Dr. Schele, who was the renowned translator of the Mayan language. Zilla was asked to work as the artist at her archeological dig sites in Mexico, Palenque and Guatemala, but had to decline the honor for personal reasons.
- 1978, slides of Zilla's sculpture, "Burdens," were selected as one of three sculptures from the state chosen for presentation at The Texas Symposium of Sculptors, at SMU in Dallas, Texas.
- Alpha Gamma Delta Sorority honored Zilla in 1978 as one of four Outstanding Women for "Contributions in the Field of

Fine Arts" by the Epsilon Delta Alumni Chapter. Harriett Nagle, President of the Board of Laguna Gloria Art Museum, presented the honor to Zilla.
• 1978, graduated UT Austin with a Bachelors in Fine Art degree, with a 3.3 grade point average.
• Zilla's graphic design career began in 1978 when she was hired by the UT College of Fine Arts and the Performing Arts Center's graphic design laboratory. Duties included directing the lab, commercial art work, book design for the UT Fine Art Museum's exhibition catalogues, publicity posters, and brochures for the art, music, drama and dance departments, as well as preparation of camera-ready copy for production, layout and paste-up. *(See additional graphics achievements in the Commercial Art/Graphic Design section.)*

TRAVEL

• New York, 1977, Zilla and Joe went to New York City with UT Professors Bill Wyman and Tommy Dale Palmore for five days, visiting 60 art Galleries and five major museums on a fact-finding tour. (In SoHo, The Hansen Gallery owner was interested in Zilla's work and asked for pieces to be sent, but the divorce prevented any action.)
• Europe, 1981, Zilla and husband, John Doonan, travelled to England, France, and Italy, visiting many private collections in numerous aristocratic homes. In London: Whitechapel: Retrospective of British 20TH Century Sculpture, Juda Gallery. Waddington Gallery: Joan Miro and Barry Flannigan, The Royal Academy of Art Japanese Edo Exhibit, Billy Keating's private collection. Paris: Andre Dunstader's private collection, Georges Pompideau Center of Fine Art, Villa Von Furstenburg: Prince Taslow Von Furstenburg's private collection. Italy: Vicenza, Villa Lambert, Countess Evelyn Kelly Lambert's private collection. Asolo: Dame Freya Stark's private collection, Villa Duse: Christian and Robert Venable's private collection, Villa Galerno: Count and Countess Di Lord's private collection, Villa Valmarana: Count Valmarana's private collection. Venice, Palazzo Barbaro: Baronesse Christina Franchetti's private collection.
• List of 26 Countries visited to date include: Mexico, Canada, the Netherlands, Italy, Austria, Luxembourg, Switzerland, Belgium, Germany, France, England, the Greek Islands, Crete, Puerto Rico, Yugoslavia, Macedonia, Slovenia, Serbia, Croatia, Liechtenstein, the Hawaiian Islands (which were, historically, a kingdom), Japan, Taiwan, Thailand, Katmandu, Nepal, Scotland, and Spain.

Foreign languages studied: Latin, Spanish, French, Italian, and Hawaiian.
• In 1987, Zilla moved to Maui, Hawaii to pursue her Fine Arts career.
• 1987, Zilla was hired as a consultant at The Village Gallery, the oldest gallery in Hawaii. She worked there more than 25 years, serving as manager for the last ten years at the Front Street location, Village Gift and Fine Art, in Lahaina, Maui. The Galleries represented 120 artists in four locations, including the Maui Ritz Hotel. Zilla's artwork was also represented and sold at these galleries.

ADDITIONAL EXHIBITIONS

• 1988, Lahaina Art Society's Group Exhibition: "Tuesday/Thursday/Twelve," featuring 75 life drawings by 12 artists from a life drawing group at George Allan's Studio. Artists: Nancy Young, George Allan, Zilla Adams, Marina Beebee, Chuck Sutherland, Lowell Mapes, Betty Hay Freeland, Pam Andelin, and others.
• 1991, Maui Art and Culture Center's "Art Maui" Exhibition, Zilla's "Light Flight" hanging plexi sculpture, 6' X 3.' The jury chose only 70 works out of 700 entries.
• 1992, Maui Art and Culture Center's "Art Maui" Exhibition, featuring Zilla's collage/plexi piece entitled "When The Rainbow Explodes," shown as the first piece at the show's entrance.
• 2010, Lahaina Art Society's Annual Photography Show included three photographs from Zilla's trip to Spain.
• Zilla's mother passed away in 2010. In 2011, she moved to Palo Alto, California, to live near son, Adam and his wife Jessica, and grandson, Avery. She earned a Masters in Clinical-Medical

Hypnotherapy in 2013, from the Palo Alto School of Hypnotherapy with over 300 training hours.
• 2011, Zilla participated in artist Andrea Fono's "Paint For Peace" event in San Francisco's "March for Peach and the Environment." Thousands of marchers connvened at City Hall to raise awareness. For the project, the public colored large mosaic pieces which were then assembled to make an 8' x 8' painting entitled "Peace." Andrea has created these mosaics in many countries, bringing people of all nationalities together for peace.
• 2013, Zilla moved to Katy, Texas, to be near her daughters and their families.
• 2015, Zilla joined Galerie Spectra, a large contemporary fine art gallery located at Memorial City Mall, Houston, Texas, and representing over 50 artists. Owner/Director, Suzanne Buckland.
• 2016, January. Zilla relocated her Healing Touch and Clinical Hypnotherapy practice to a Katy, Texas, office at 439 Mason Park, Blvd, Bldg. C, Suite B, Katy, Texas 77450. In addition to her art career, she has been practicing energy medicine since 1995 and her additional healing modalities include Reiki and EFT Trauma Release techniques.
• 2015, Zilla finished a three-month photo project, completing a professional photographic record of her artwork, totalling over 1,400 images.
• 2015, began writing her autobiographical art book on June 26th, and finished the first draft in October of that year.
• 2016, Zilla was chosen as Galerie Spectra's "Artist of the Month" and this exhibit, May 13 through June 9, was her Sixth Solo Show, featuring 30 monoprints and paintings.
• 2016, three works exhibited at The Earth, Sky and Space Fine Art Exhibition, May 15th, the first ever held at NASA, the Johnson Space Center, Houston, Texas. Arranged by Galerie Spectra of Houston, with over 30 local artists participating.

GALLERY/STUDIO AFFILIATIONS

• Ann Morehead Gallery, Houston, Texas
• Gallery 600, Austin, Texas
• The Bird's Eye Review, Houston, Texas
• Beverly Hayden's Gallery, Austin, Texas
• Art Graphics Gallery, Hearne, Texas
• The Village Galleries, Lahaina, Maui, Hawaii
• 2013, Zilla moved to Katy, Texas.
• 2014, Zilla joined Armando Rodriguez's Fine Art Studio in Houston, Texas, named "Taller ISMA." sharing a large building with six other fine artists, and working in mixed-media, including printmaking, painting, collage, watercolor, and oil.

PROFESSIONAL COMMISSIONS & PRIVATE COLLECTIONS

• Hill Country Pools
• Dr. Raleigh Ross, MD
• Schill Steel Company
• Montrose Children's Clinic
• A.D. Stenger, Architecture
• John and Ann Heyburn
• The Austin Law Firm
• Chaparral Productions
• Valve Corporation of America
• Joseph Esposito, curator of the Poster Collections at the Museum of Modern Art, New York City.
• Ginny Volterra, Rome, Italy
• Since 1987, Zilla's art works have sold at the Village Galleries to clients from all over the world.

ORGANIZATIONS/TEACHING

• The National Museum of Women in the Arts, Washington, DC
• The Art League of Houston, Texas
• The Fine Art Museum of Houston, Texas
• The Metropolitan Museum of Art, New York, NY
• The San Francisco Museum of Modern Art, CA
• The Pacific Art League, Palo Alto, CA
• "P.O.P.", Peninsula Outdoor Painters (Plein Air) Group, CA
• The Hui Noeau Fine Arts Center, Maui, Hawaii
• The "MAC" Maui Arts and Culture Center and Museum,

Maui, Hawaii
- ACVAA, Austin Contemporary Visual Arts Association, co-founder.
- Official Docent of the University of Texas Fine Art Museum, Huntington and Michener Galleries, Austin, Texas
- Lecture on "Women in Art History" to Porter Junior High School Honors English Program, Austin, Texas
- Costume Design, Austin Civic Ballet and Austin Ballet Theater
- Teaching experience: The Country Day School, Austin, Texas, Sunset Valley Elementary School, Austin, Wolman Elementary, Katy, Texas, The School at Sherwood Forest, Houston, Texas

COMMERCIAL ART & GRAPHIC DESIGN

- 1962, *Texas Buiilder Magazine*, illustrations and cover design.
- *The Texas Journal of Heating, Plumbing, and Contracting*, artwork.
- The Texas Education Agency, Austin, illustrating, teaching visual aids to teachers.
- The Civil Defense Department, art work.
- 1963, The State of Texas Comptroller's Department, State Capitol, Austin, Texas. Created visual aids, charts, etc., for Governor John Connally.
- 1971, Arthur Barr Productions, CA, squirrel illustrations for educational documentary film by "Red" and Marjorie Adams, entitled "Where Should A Squirrel Live?"
- 1973, UT department of Portuguese, illustrations.
- 1974, The Greater Texas Industrial Supply Company, Inc., artwork.
- 1978, UT College of Fine Arts and Performing Arts Center Graphic Design Laboratory, Artist II full-time, Director, book design, exhibition catalogues, publicity for the Art, Music, Dance and Drama Departments production work.
- The Education Services Center, Region XIII, painting, "The Genius", used in a film on creativity called "Beyond Awareness." The etching entitled: "The Cry," was also used for secondary school curriculum lesson plans.
- The Texas Circuit, logo design for nonprofit literary organization for writers and small publishers.
- 1980, *The Solar Energy Society and Bulletin*, 12 pages, bi-monthly, Russel Smith, executive director.
- Good Right Arm Advertising Agency, freelance production.
- Moore and More Advertising Agency, art work, illustration, and production. Roy Crouse, Art Director.
- Canson and Associates, illustration for highway safety program and the Jaycee's.
- Adams and Adams Films, art work, paste-up, and illustration.
- Texas Society of Bioenergetic Analysis, graphic design for Dr. Barry King, Phd.
- Louisiana State University Press, illustrations of Bertolt Brecht and Samuel Beckett for cover design of book entitled *Meditations,* by Martin Esslin.
- Louisiana State University Press, cover illustration for dust jacket for *Flannery O'Connor's Dark Comedies*, by Carol Shloss.
- *Texas Monthly* magazine, production department staff position. Betty Moore, director, Mike Levy, publisher, Bill Broyles, Jr., editor. Duties: processing ads, specifying type, layout, mechanicals, negatives, color checking, graphics, and production of special sections, and for the circulation and promotion departments.
- Marsh and Box Real Estate, design for *Texas Monthly* ad.
- Log Homes, Inc., design for *Texas Monthly* ad.
- *Texas Monthly*, production for "The 1980 Christmas Gift Guide", 4-color spread, 16 page advertising section for December Issue.
- Carnival Brasilero, a poster illustration, newspaper ad, and T-shirt design.
- Education Service Center, Region XIII, logo design for an educational publication.
- 1981, *Texas Solar Energy Society*, a 28 page Newspaper, Russel Smith, Director.
- Sagebrush Studio, production of promotional posters, newsletters, and "Pockets of Influence" for *Texas Monthly*.
- Thunderco brochure for Rick Eddrington.
- Rooster Andrews ad for Roy Crouse, Moore and More advertising agency.
- Texas Monthly Press, production of *Guide to Mexico*, designed

by Janice Ashford (now Janice Shay).
• Texas Monthly Press, complete book design, dust jacket, and cover illustration for the novel, *A Family Likeness,* by Janice Stout. This novel won the Frank Wardlaw prize for literature.
• Solar Energy Society membership directory, for Russel Smith.
• *Texas Highways* magazine, design and illustration.
• *Texas Monthly* magazine, design for Cindy Stone, circulation director.
• Louisiana State University Press, cover illustration of an African woman for novel, *Massinni,* by Tidiane Dem, translated by Frances Frenaye. It won the Pegasus Prize for Literature.
• *Texas Monthly,* the "Christmas Gift Guide" and "Cactus, Cowboy Boots" posters for promotion department.
• Sagebrush Studio. Zilla opened her own office as an associate artist, with Janice Ashford, Tom Curry, Roberta Hill, Ellen Simmons, Michael Knott, and Kathi Branson. llustration, graphic design, book design, advertising design, production work.
• Walter Carrington Builder, designed and prepared their real estate brochures.
• *Austin Homes & Gardens* magazine, designed real estate ads.
• *Texas Monthly*, "The Texas/California Report", illustrations.
• Texas Monthly Press, paste-up for *The Guide to Texas*.
• Travis State School for the Deaf, illustration and brochure.
• Bureau of Business Research, design for *The Directory of Texas Manufacturers.*
• Rooster Andrews, "Orange Fever" ad campaign.
• Ray Hall Advertising Agency, illustrations for Killeen Mall.
• *Texas Monthly*, the "Christmas Gift Kit," circulation.
• Russel E. Smith Enterprises, business papers, logo design.
• *Texas Insuror* magazine, graphics and paste-up, 80 pages.
• Tom Curry, Sagebrush Studio, artwork and illustrations.
• *Database Monthly* magazine, circulation design for Jackie Petit.
• Texas Solar Energy Society, design and preparation of their *Spectra Directory.*
• West Austin Skyline project for Ellen Simmons.
• *Austin Insights* magazine, format design for Paul Rheinlander, publisher.
• *Condominiums and Townhomes Magazine*, art direction, full-page ad for Julia and Rich Finney, Publishers.
• John Byram Properties, double-page ad for the Congress Square Project.
• USA Olympic Committee, Bicycling Team T-shirt design, used for their fundraiser.
• Data Base Publications, hired as production manager/art director for two Magazines: *Database Monthly*, a 68-page tabloid computer trade journal for the Data General Computer community, and *Online Data Access* magazine, a 48-page tabloid for Wang Computer community. Responsibilities included hiring, training staff, production, design and redesign magazines, budgeting, printer liaison, circulation and marketing design, illustration, and even cartooning.
1984, moved freelance studio to Bulian Lane, West Lake Hills, Austin.
• Database Publications, designed Wang business reply card, for Sharon park.
• Austin Ballet Theater, designed class schedule.
• Texas Solar Energy Society, designed *Sunburst* newsletter logo design.
• Texas Dental Association, illustration for dental convention program.
• Database Publications, "The Data Store Directory," direct mail package design.
• Carlos Femat Advertising Agency, annual report production and layout.
• *Texas Insuror* magazine, production and paste-up of magazine.

COMMERCIAL ART HONORS

• 1981, Award of Excellence, Texas School Public Relations Association, communications contest for "Beyond Awareness" film illustration.
• Award of Merit, Texas School Public Relations Association's communications contest for information brochure.